Busi

Impact.

Brand.

FROM IDEA TO INNOVATION:

INSPIRING SOCIAL

ENTREPRENEURSHIP.

By James Jay Mawaka

Business. Impact. Brand by James Jay Mawaka
Copyright © James Mawaka 2018

Printed in the United Kingdom
ISBN: 978-1790-178179 (Paperback)

Printed in United Kingdom
First printing 2018. Published by Lenoir Publishing

www.lenoirfoundation.com

DEDICATION

Dedicated to the pessimist sees the difficulty in
every opportunity; an optimist that sees the
opportunity in every difficulty.

Table of Contents

JAMES JAY MAWAKA

Foreword

What is the impact you want to make in the world?

We live in era of entrepreneurship, and you most probably may be an entrepreneur, the question is what kind of entrepreneur are you? And why you do what you do?

I have to say that in the last 7 to 10 years of my life I met so many entrepreneurs, being honest none of them like Jay, he is a real entrepreneur who can guide anyone to succeed in becoming a social entrepreneur. He is a leader, he has a mission, a vision and the most important he has a story and he wants to live his life based on leaving a legacy for the next generation of entrepreneurs. How he decides to do that? Through education, that's why he came with the idea of writing this inspirational guide on how to make an impact, how to brand and do business.

When Jay approached me to mentor him on his book journey, I could see already whatever he told me about this book even if back then was only an idea. I say NO to often of taking people on a journey of writing their dream book, but in Jay's case I had to say YES! Based on what? Intuition, I believe this is the key, in life and business. I am so proud of YOU, Jay. Your passion for education and sharing great worth ideas with others will lead you to the top. You are a dreamer, a challenger, a leader.

This book; 'Business. Impact. Brand' is a step by step formula designed to help you succeed in your social entrepreneurial journey. Why this book is a must read?

Firstly, this book is full of strategies and techniques to show you the way, how to do it, what you need to know to make the right decision on making the impact you want in your business. Jay's approach will help you with clarity and tools to stay on the right path.

Secondly, the power of all the research he has done on other successful social entrepreneurs who already are there where you want to be. His dedication is worthy enough to make you succeed by offering you the right information and ways of doing your best in this journey.

Thirdly, in this book he shares inspirational and transformational story on how he went from idea to innovation, from dreams to results, from 'I wish' to 'I do' attitude. In this book he is sharing with us his personal and professional journey and we all can take notes and put in practice his advices, steps, tips, strategies and tools to help us to become the social entrepreneur we always wanted to be.

Now I ask you again: what is the impact you want to make in the world? If you are serious about it, in: 'Business. Impact. Brand' you will find the answer because in this book, Jay is sharing with us how he went from idea to real success with his social enterprise Lenoir Foundation. Your success in life and business has to be specific, measurable, accountable, realistic, and managed in time. In this book you will find it all those steps.

Ungureanu Ionut Iulian

Author |Speaker | Coach

The founder & CEO of Raise the World Company.

This book is for you if......

- *You want to make a change.*
- *You believe in yourself and want to fight for your dreams.*
- *You do not rely on the government for social change.*
- *Want to turn awareness into action.*
- *You work hard because you love the work you do.*
- *You want to start a company that is driving change every day with their services, programs, or products.*
- *You want to make decisions that drive social change, because you give a shit.*

PREFACE

BEING A SOCIAL ENTREPNEUR, AN INBORN TRAIT?

When we consider the risks, pains, and commitments involved in being a social entrepreneur, we usually feel we do not have the capacity of being one. Owing to this, some of us drop our dreams of owning our own social enterprises. Some also believe that social entrepreneurial skills are transferred genetically.

Let us examine it this way, are there people born to be employees? No, nobody is born to be either an employee or an entrepreneur. As much as these two roles are socially important, I can say emphatically that not everyone would be entrepreneurs and not everyone would be employees. This is because the chief executive officer of a company is of the same level of importance as the security personnel at the gate of his company. The chief executive officer cannot perform the role of the security personnel along with his.

General education practices have trained the heart of men to obey laws, never to question the things they see, the statement "just do as you are told" is now being followed and it is now the way we pattern our lives. To be great entrepreneurs, few things we have learned in schools might need to be unlearned. An example of such is the fact that we are taught in schools to see the challenges before the opportunities. As entrepreneurs, we have to take a look at the opportunities in a situation as we unravel the challenges.

This is not to say that school practices are bad. Rather, we are saying some things learned in the four walls of the classroom might not necessarily apply in the world of business. Many stick to these rules and end up frustrated as they struggle to have their heads above the waters in the business world.

Many do not follow their dreams of becoming entrepreneurs or even struggle as entrepreneurs because they have been used to being told what to do. As social entrepreneurs, we decide who we employ, what to pay our employee. Social entrepreneurs are problem solvers, they do not wait to take orders but rather they give orders. They are risk takers going through the path less travelled.

In life, failures are indicators that we did something, we might not have done it well, but it teaches us better ways to do that thing. We have been taught that failing is bad, but the truth is our perspective of failure is what might either be bad or good.

Many refuse to pursue their dreams as social entrepreneurs because they do not want to fail. They fear the word 'failure'; they fear what people would say if they do not make headway in the business they have set out to do. They associate pleasure to not starting their businesses than the pleasure they would probably get from starting and succeeding as entrepreneurs. Some social entrepreneurs leave their businesses small and stagnant because they associate more pleasure to being able to oversee their business than having more hands doing the works for them, they fear taking risks.

The first step to succeeding as social entrepreneurs believes in our ideas, selling the ideas to individuals who would key into it. For example, have you seen anyone who is employed to market Honda products, but he uses Toyota vehicles? Such a person cannot or may not be able to sell the product effectively. This is because he might not be able to convince people to patronize him or buy his products. The secret behind this is that you cannot market what you do not believe in and the very first work of an entrepreneur is to sell his idea to people by convincing them about his product.

Starting out as kids, our handwritings did not become legible the first day we started writing. However, as we continued writing, with constant practice, we improved steadily and got really good overtime. This principle also applies in the business world; we are not yet failures until we decide in our hearts that we have failed.

This book is aimed at showing you how to successfully start, and run a social enterprise using the business-impact-brand method. Join me as I unravel how to do this.

WHY?

*"You Don't Have To Be the Best
to Create Something Impactful"*

Over the last few years, as I have started up one exciting project after another, I have often thought that my life could not get any better. In writing this book, however, I have come to realise that I have been on a dummy run, preparing myself for the greatest challenge and opportunity of my lifetime. In this book, I want to share not only my story, but the great stories of people I have met in my social enterprise journey that are already leading the way. I have learnt a great deal from these visionaries. I hope this will help you learn from the successes and the occasional failures I have faced along the way.

I have written this book for the new wave of emerging social entrepreneurs who have a different perspective from politicians and many business leaders. The people that have a dream to build organisations at the same time make a living while helping people and transforming their communities from the small townships in South Africa and to the small sectors in India.

All my life I have thrived on new opportunities and challenges, that is what drives me, be it personal or academic. Writing this book has been a huge challenge for me because I feel it's very important to share the knowledge I have acquired throughout the years in my journey. This book will show you how to go from I wish I could help, to I know I can help. To go from "I have an idea" to unleashing and executing your ideas. The truth is ordinary people have the power to change the world and in this book, I want you to learn what you can do and as NIKE would say: Just do it!

"I know it can be done because I did it myself "

My family was modest, and my parents ensured that they provided the very best they could despite all the challenges they faced. Over the years I have realised no matter where a person is headed our values, beliefs and attitudes are influenced a great deal by our childhood. I come from a highly academic and opinionated family. Through them, I have learnt the value of taking responsibility, good work ethic, aiming high and open-mindedness

As I look back today, I was always around entrepreneurs who also held normal 9-5 jobs on the side. My mother worked as a bookkeeper by day, at night she was on her singer machine sewing, cutting and stitching together the latest outfit for her retail shop. On the other hand, my father well-educated laboratory technician also made ends meet by selling vegetables to traders at the local market.

I was a fledgling entrepreneur by the age of 10.

I had never heard of the word entrepreneur, I just wanted to make extra money for lunch. I was the kid at school selling the latest Nintendo Gameboy. I never owned one for more than two weeks, I had to sell it to make a profit and buy the next one with a new cartridge. During the summer holidays business was booming, with temperatures reaching 32 Degrees Celsius I figured this would be a great time to sell ice lollies to the local kids. There was no need for a business plan; it was a no-brainer. I had a simple process, buy low at wholesale price and sell high, then repeat the process over and over again while saving my profits. I nurtured a secret ambition to be a businessman. This was partly fuelled by my obsession with cars, particularly German cars. This was further encouraged a few years later when I had the chance to work at my sister's motor body shop, selling car parts over the counter was an experience like no other. I might not have been the best employee and was reluctant to get my hands dirty at times, but I was brimming with confidence and had a thirst for knowledge. I learnt to embrace diverse personalities and negotiation skills which as a result have greatly boosted my confidence and decision-making skills today.

As an adolescent I moved to the UK permanently with my mother and two sisters, an event which was a major turning point in my young life as it changed my perception on how I viewed various issues I was now considered a refugee, a stateless person; I had left everything behind, I was torn apart.

My first day of school I couldn't communicate at first. My English was really good, so it wasn't language that was the problem – it was self-esteem. I had very low self-esteem because I was an asylum seeker, deep down I wanted to express my true identity. With help from my family, I had to learn to navigate complex systems and get the support I needed, every day I reminded myself that I am not only young, I am talented, have aspirations and dreams.

When I meet new people and tell them my story they ask me all sorts of questions: What was it like on your first day? How did it feel to have to wait for life to begin because you couldn't get to go to school immediately, go to university or find a job until you got your papers? How did you navigate through life at a young age? I always say when you move to a new country, you don't know anything about life there, but you just have to adapt. yes, I was torn apart, it felt like life as I knew it was taken from me. Every day I think about home, I have many memories: studying at my desk, watching films, evenings with my family, the beautiful sunsets. Leaving my country ... In the beginning it was very difficult, but with the help of my family and friends – I have integrated.

Looking back, my mother set me on a path to being

adventurous and self-sufficient and to being considerate to others. She always preached that I can achieve whatever I set my mind too provided I put in the work required., but what really motivated me to become the person I am today was my desire to become successful and build an organisation that would uplift communities and those around me.

"Yes, aim to be extremely successful. Learn the best tools and techniques. But have your heart focused on these objectives. It's worth the fight to empower the poorest."

~Lord Dr Michael Hastings CBE

Having at least the foundations of a more formal education, having good manners and respect for other people's ideas and for each other and broadening your outlook is very important in shaping the person you eventually become. During my final year at university I met Martin Luther King III an American human rights advocate and community activist. He is the oldest son and oldest living child of civil rights leaders Martin Luther King Jr. Just like his father he is very well spoken, composed and has a very unique way of inspiring people. It was him who inspired me to set up my first social enterprise, it was the moment when I got the opportunity to pose for a quick picture with him: we spark up a conversation, we spoke about the current state of civil rights movement, his father's involvement and how hard it must be to follow in the footsteps of such a great man. I have always been curious about people regardless of their background, asking a question is a good way to learn. During our conversation I told him a bit about myself and where I am from, he asked what my hope and expectations for the people in Africa. That afternoon on my way home it dawned on me that all my role models from Barack Obama, Martin Luther king Jr, Elon Musk and Alan Turing just to name a few all had something in common that stood out, they had a spirit of hope. There is a moment in their lives were that spirit of hopefulness has had to come through and has enabled them to make their mark on history despite the odds they were facing. This brief conversation changed my life in a way, it made me believe that ordinary people can do extraordinary things; it gave me a sense of what direction I would take with my life.

Despite everything that I had gone through and challenges I had faced, it was that audacity of hope that kept me going and I also owe a debt to those that invested and gave me opportunities.

In May 2015 I drafted my first plan on starting a social enterprise. I had a part time job and naturally I was unhappy, and I was complaining about my job every day. My world was shrouded with a giant cloud of negativity. I knew something had to change. This was not how I wanted to live my life. It took a while to make the shift from worrying about what I wanted to "be" instead want I wanted to "do". This is a common mistake young people make, when you are more concerned with what you want to be then you might succeed but when you get there you will most likely feel empty or when you don't get there you will have nothing to show for it. But if you are worrying about having an impact or improving society the person you become and the skills you acquire in the process is going to be worthwhile.

Using what knowledge, I gathered on google and numerous masterclasses on charities and social enterprises and the belief that people are generally good if you give them the opportunities they will do the right thing. I also took up activities that pushed my boundaries and constantly ventured out of my comfort zone. This entire "exercise" of pushing boundaries helped me to be comfortable with the uncomfortable. It allowed me to learn to go with the flow, to adapt and to not let fear stop me from moving forward.

The greatest lesson I've learnt is that if you close your eyes tight and just force yourself to take that step forward; you'd open your eyes to a new adventure. I finally took a blind leap of faith and quit my job, trusting that the universe wouldn't screw me over and my stars will somehow align and took another leap to start my own social enterprise. "Lenoir Foundation" an organisation purely setup for education and entrepreneurship. It was an idea that came about after hearing time and again on how aid from the west was not helping instead it just holds down people longer than it should. These people didn't want charity, they wanted choices in life. One of my favourite philanthropist and life coach Tony Robbins states in his book Unlimited Power "The best way to help poor people is to be a model of possibilities, to let them know there is another set of choices available and to assist them in developing the resources to become self-sufficient".

That is why with Lenoir Foundation I decided to focus on Economic empowerment and education. Ultimately, it's providing empowerment to local people, so they can start developing their own economies.

Through economic empowerment with microfinance loans, businesses are set up, individuals prosper, and families are provided for. By giving access to funds, communities are able to increase productivity and lift themselves out of poverty. Our support doesn't end with finance. We also ensure that growth is nurtured by providing skills training in small business management and other areas. Sponsoring education, our sponsorship programme is a fantastic and rewarding way to directly help a child get a head-start in life. In fact, most of the students in our scholarship programme are female and this makes us even more certain that about having an impact. It has been shown time and time again that when you raise a young woman above the poverty line, you change the whole destiny of her family for good.

The Business Impact Brand method aims to provide tactical advice for anyone that has the desire and is determined to start solving big social problems they care about. This guide also has a social bent, as I had the chance to talk with countless social entrepreneurs during the course of writing it. Social entrepreneurs face a special challenge that for-profit entrepreneurs do not experience. No venture capitalists are throwing money at them. The needs of a social entrepreneur's users are different, which results in different business models. As a student I figured out, starting an organization is an empowering way to create wealth and add value to your community and the world we live in. Step by step I will take you on a journey on how to go from idea to innovation

PART ONE

WHAT IS A SOCIAL ENTERPRISE

"My dream is to find individuals who take financial resources and convert them into changing the world in the most positive ways."

- Jeff Skoll

INTRODUCTION

We all want to be successful in what we do. Whatever is worth doing is worth doing well, right? As entrepreneurs, we aim at growing our business to become social enterprises. In other to achieve this we have to first understand what a social enterprise is.

Some people start businesses to improve the quality of their life, others seek to work for themselves, and some simply see an opportunity in the market that they can't resist.

But sometimes the thing that tickles the entrepreneurial spirit in you is the desire to use business as a means of creating positive change. Such businesses are called social enterprises.

This is called "social entrepreneurship", and it's an approach to business that's gaining in popularity as globalization brings conversations about sustainability and international development to a global stage, and more people ask themselves, "What can I do for the world today?"

Social entrepreneurship involves starting mission-based social enterprises that dedicate some or even all of their profits toward furthering a cause—giving their customers a purpose behind every purchase.

"Social entrepreneurship" has a very broad definition that can arguably include non-profit organizations like

Doctors Without Borders, which rely almost exclusively on donations and grants, and even for-profit companies like Tesla that put their clean energy products front and center.

A social enterprise is a type of business where the bottom line and success metrics are measured in more than just profits. Instead, social enterprises typically measure success based on a triple bottom line:

People: The social impact of your business, and your ability to change lives and develop a community in a sustainable way.

Planet: Your environmental impact; how you contribute to a sustainable planet or reduce the carbon footprint (CO_2 emissions) of your business and customers.

Profit: Like traditional businesses, they need to make money in order to sustain themselves, pay workers and grow as an enterprise.

Social Entrepreneurship is about harnessing commerce for a cause.

For this reason, one of the challenges to succeeding in social entrepreneurship is that it's easy to measure profit (did you make money, or did you not make money?), but it's not as easy to measure your impact on people or the planet and communicate it to others.

Social entrepreneurs adopt a business model that puts their mission at the center, and are held accountable to their customers and stakeholders based on their proposed impact.

For today's consumers and businesses, social responsibility is a growing priority as concerns about climate change, international development, and supply chain ethics become a more prominent topic of international discussion.

In a survey by Social Enterprise UK, 1 in 3 people said they feel ashamed about buying from socially irresponsible businesses. In another study, 91% of global consumers expected companies to operate responsibly, and address social and environmental issues.

This reflects a shift in consumer awareness about the impact of their purchase decisions. Not only are businesses being held to a higher standard, but many consumers are holding themselves to a higher standard as well.

So, while social enterprises, by definition, must dedicate a portion of their profits to the impact they want to make, they do enjoy the following benefits that help them succeed:

Mission-based branding: A company story with a cause at its core makes consumers feel good about every purchase they make from you.

Partnership opportunities: A social enterprise, because of their mission-based motivations, can partner with other non-profit organizations and for-profit companies to leverage existing audiences and established reputations to create a presence in their market. "In kind" resources and discounts are not uncommon for social enterprises.

Press coverage: Publications and blogs love to cover social enterprises and their impact, helping them to evangelize their efforts and share their impact.

Certifications and support systems: Social enterprises can be eligible for grants, "impact investing" opportunities that focus on job creation and sustainability, and special certifications such as a Benefit Corporation status that make it easier to establish credibility, commit to transparency, and attract customers, employees, volunteers, and investors.

For the sake of this piece, we'll look at what it takes to create a sustainable for-profit social enterprise. And that starts, as most businesses do, with figuring out what you want to sell.

A social enterprise is a business organization whose sole aim has gone beyond just making profits; it uses its resources to serve the society and makes profits at the long run. A social enterprise is a business organization which satisfies the needs of its customers, by adding values, producing quality goods and services which are reliable and trustworthy, at the same time caters for the needs of its workers and shareholders.

Social enterprises are also involved in nonprofit duties; they sometimes get involved in charitable works like providing health facilities, pipe borne water, youth empowerment programs, poverty alleviation programs and so on.

In this section, we would be discussing the four key steps, which we can use as entrepreneurs to transform our businesses into social enterprises.

- Get clear on your mission
- Finding funding
- Develop a culture of measurement
- Make mistakes

CHAPTER ONE

GET CLEAR ON YOUR MISSION

"Don't ask what the world needs. Ask what makes you come alive and go do it. Because what the world needs is people who have come alive."

~Howard Thurman

Starting a business entailed several things. As social entrepreneurs, we have to first count our costs, ask ourselves where we are aiming at. It is a well-known saying that if we do not know where we are going, we would not know when we have reached there.

Our preparation determines where we might likely be in the business world few years from when we started. Adequate preparation is needed to start and groom a business therefore we have to be cleared on our mission, what we do want our business to be like.

Why should you be a Social Entrepreneur?

We need to identify our reason for doing things so as to clearly define our mission in doing that thing. This is especially true with social enterprises. Many start their own business because they want to be independent; they know it feels good to say "I am the CEO of this company"; things go my way around here. They want to dictate the time they get to work, they want to be their own boss, all these are good but this all there is to be an entrepreneur? No, there are many more commitments far from feeling good or just wanting to be your own boss.

Social entrepreneur's takers. Most times, they do things that are not reasonable to people and even themselves, they love adventures and are not afraid that risk or adventures they take might not end well.

Social entrepreneurs are first servants before they become leaders; they are people who burn with passion. They see a need in the society and try to satisfy it. It takes more than just being a boss to be a great social entrepreneur, it takes being committed to knowing that our lives and that of others depends on our actions and inactions.

Social Entrepreneurs are people of passion. Passion for change is the first quality that all social enterprise founders start with before embarking on a journey to raise awareness, grow funding, solve problems and meet needs. A social enterprise is a for-profit company that has two goals - achieve social, cultural community good and to generate revenue in order to sustain itself, sans donations and grants.

Essentially, social entrepreneurs earn their living by making a positive change.

The best social companies began with the founders' passion for change.

If there's a social or environmental or justice problem that has affected you personally or someone you love or goes against or is aligned with your core values, and you want to use entrepreneurship to bring it to life, you must do your homework. I'm not talking about spreadsheets and profit margins. You need to know exactly what is being done already because you don't want to take away resources from an existing social enterprise doing great work; and you also want to use your time and resources wisely.

Before thinking about building a business plan or legally incorporating, conduct a SWOT analysis upfront in order to develop your competitive advantage. You want to do something niche-specific. And finally, what's your story? Why do you want to work in said space? Your story will differentiate you.

The mission comes first for social entrepreneurs, but that doesn't eclipse the importance of having a quality product to sell. After all, when all is said and done, a for-profit social enterprise needs to make money to survive just like any other business.

But there's a pattern amongst successful social enterprises of establishing a good "product-cause fit" that aligns their mission with what they sell.

For social enterprises, their mission is a competitive advantage that can help them stand out in a crowded market—if they can communicate their motivation and the impact they can make.

Many social enterprises adopt a model where they donate a portion of profits to a cause, but that's not the only way to position your company as a social enterprise.

It's not just saying, 'Hey, we have a social mission as an organization, and X percent of our sales goes to nonprofit X, Y, and Z.' I think it needs to be deeper and more authentic than that.

There are also social enterprises that focus on:

Creating jobs within the communities they care about, such as hiring local ex-convicts or ethically outsourcing production to communities in need of fair work and career development opportunities.

Reducing their carbon footprint by planting trees or going out of their way to reduce carbon emissions throughout their entire supply chain and educating customers about it.

Hosting workshops and "people development" initiatives to teach skills and empower people to build better lives for themselves and their communities.

Advocating for diversity and inclusion on behalf of underrepresented groups and becoming an engine of inspiration, such as Goldie Blox does by making toys to expose young girls to the joys of engineering.

Transparency and sustainable impact are essential for a successful social enterprise. And these things are easier to achieve if your cause is close to your heart and you choose an impact that you can measure.

"Integrity is doing the right thing, even when no one is watching," in the words of C.S Lewis.

Transparency is about visibly demonstrating your integrity and holding yourself accountable to your mission and the people who support it.

Depending on your mission, you can directly implement your plans for change as a social entrepreneur and expand your contributions as you grow. But if you choose to partner with non-profit organizations (NPOs) to help execute the "social" part of your social enterprise (as many do), be sure to do your homework before you reach out and ask questions like:

- What am I ultimately giving back to?
- How will my contributions actually be used and what are the organization's operating costs?
- How does the organization measure its success?
- Is their impact sustainable or will it only end up doing more harm in the long run?
- Does this organization have an ethical history as a non-profit?

This is all part of your founding story—the tale of why you started your business—and will likely come up again and again in your elevator pitch, About Page, PR efforts and more. So, refine it with your mission in mind and your action plan for creating change.

Social entrepreneurship isn't the only way a business can be for-benefit and not just for-profit.

Many companies own their social responsibility based on a growing belief that those with the power to do so can and should try to make the world a better place.

Our connected world has brought about a new era of awareness, where we can find problems to solve and lives to improve across the street or across the world if we choose.

People from all over are making the decision to make change in whatever way they can, whether it's by being more conscious of what they buy as consumers or building an engine for social and environmental good by becoming entrepreneurs.

Business is not a game of cards; you should not start a business without having a blueprint. As entrepreneurs, we should have a set plan. A vision of what we want our business to be known for, our culture.

Many social entrepreneurs make the mistake of not writing down the main purpose of the business and Myles Munroe once said, "when the purpose of a thing is unknown abuse is inevitable." If we do not define in clear terms the purpose of our social enterprise, we would be swayed by the waves of time and events, we would not have a focus, and this leads to lack of growth in business, especially social enterprises.

It is not enough to just have a blueprint; a blueprint without reference is as good as being thrown away. We should always refer back to our blueprint, we should take time to go through it, follow the trend of growth of the business so as to stay in line. As the trend of things changes, it is our duty as entrepreneurs to recognize our blueprint, adding and removing something from it to make it fit into the current trend of things.

YOUR MISSION STATEMENT

The best way to start is by deciding who we want to serve, where we want to serve them and how we want to serve them. As social entrepreneurs who want to make impact, we would have to be sure of the problems we would like to solve with our products or services.

The mission statement helps to focus our minds to the things or values our business encompasses, it also helps focus the minds of our employees, clients and investors on our areas of specialization. The mission statement does not necessarily have to be a long write up; it is supposed to be a short, easy to memorize and remember piece.

In order to get the true value of our social enterprise so as to use it to provide a mission statement, the following questions would be of great use. What service do I want to provide? Why do I choose this service? What solutions would it provide? For example, if a medical doctor who is planning to setup his owns hospital as a social enterprise or one who already own an hospital is to answer these questions, he might say, "what service do I want to give? I would like to save life with my knowledge of medicine, what service would I like to provide? I would care for the sick; making their lives a top priority before money, what service do I want to give? Help the poor access good health services at little cost. From these, his mission statement could be derived. "We save your life and save your money". This has helped summarize his aim, the reason for the existence of his social enterprise hospital.

There is no field we would like to go into that is a monopoly. There are people who have gone ahead of us, people who started before us. It is important to learn about the horizon we want to work in, the people in the industry and how they influence the world.

It is important to know that in all industries, there are businesses that soar while some struggle to find their feet. As social entrepreneurs, in order to make headway in an industry it is better to study the principles that guilds these two categories.

Learning about why the companies that struggles still struggles and why those that soar are soaring helps us to build our culture, the way we want our businesses to be addressed, the pattern in which we would like our business to follow.

This research is important to entrepreneurs because it helps us know the likely challenges we might face, those that the other companies have faced and how they came through it. It also helps to broaden our hearts and understanding about the likely challenges we might face.

You would also need an action plan.

An action plan helps a social entrepreneur breakdown his large goals into smaller units in a to-do task manner. A social entrepreneur needs to commit himself to this action plan which should include a deadline.

Your action plan acts as your manual, it is your guide. It must be built around your daily, weekly and even hourly goals. The action plan helps social entrepreneurs to act consciously and makes them goal oriented it serves a drive that pushes him/her out of his/her comfort zone.

As a social entrepreneur, you need to convince people to trust you—to fund you, to invest their time, to leave better paying jobs to support your cause. "You need to clearly articulate a problem and the solution. It's easier to engage supporters when you make it clear how your organization is part of that solution.

For example, there are approximately 15 million refugees worldwide, and the majority are stuck in limbo: they can't return home, and they can't survive safely where they are. A social enterprise aimed at helping refugees can choose to provide lasting solutions for the most vulnerable refugees by permanently relocating them to a new country where they can rebuild safely, or, when possible, enabling them to integrate into their host country.

FINDING CAPITAL

"Build relationships over time… explore your options… and fund yourself if you can."

~ Dmitry Selitskiy

To start a social enterprise or keep a social enterprise running, providing financial resources to keep the business running, funding is a very important aspect of business. Without proper means of funding, the business might soon go bankrupt.

Many social entrepreneurs go out of business while many intending social entrepreneurs do not even start their businesses because of the fear of not having enough money to fund the social enterprise.

MONEY AS A SCARCE COMMODITY

Many do what they do because the pay is high and not because they have passion for it. Money is a scarce commodity, it is never enough, and we can never get enough of it to satisfy our needs or wants. The rich acquires more of it, the poor strive to have it in their possession.

Many want to be the boss of themselves, to determine their own cash flow. Many social entrepreneurs and intending entrepreneurs get stuck because of lack of money.

Money is not real, it is an illusion that has been designed to look real to humans, and it helps solve problems and has also helped create several problems in the human society. It helps us to access goods and services freely without necessarily carrying bulky things. Money goes beyond the physical cash we carry in our pockets.

As social entrepreneurs, in order to finance our businesses and move from scratch to the level of impact, we desire we have to understand that fund raising goes beyond raising money to finance our business. Although, raising money is also part of fund raising.

MY IDEA, MY FUND

The first fund a social entrepreneur has at hand for his social enterprise is his idea, what he has to offer. You may be surprised at the angle at which I am taking this, but the truth is that the most important fund of a social enterprise is the concept on which the business is built upon.

Most times, we seek funds as liquid cash, but fund is anything that can at the long run sustain the growth of a business. The way we present our ideas as social entrepreneurs or intending entrepreneurs determines the amount of funds we raise for the business.

Have you ever asked why banks and other financial institutions request for proposals when seeking business loans? The main reason why proposals are important is to be sure of the ideas in which the business is built. Many a time, we discover that most people's concepts are good; they have brilliant ideas but why is it that they are being turned down? The way we present our ideas also determines the level of growth the idea would receive.

As social entrepreneurs, in order to successfully raise funds for our business we have to first raise the standard of the idea that initiates the business.

MY PASSION MY FUND

As social entrepreneurs, our passion, the belief we have in our ideas helps us in raising funds for our business. You may ask how? Like I said earlier in the preface, you cannot market a product you do not believe in.

Passion is most important in growing a business, passion goes beyond doing something for money, when we are passionate about our businesses, we put all our efforts and do it without stress, and we endure the immediate pains and challenges in other to see our business grow.

Most businesses do not grow because from the first day of the business, the entrepreneurs work towards self-gratification even at the expense of the business growth, many instead of reinvesting the profits they get from the business back in order to build the business they rather spend the money in grooming and satisfying their selfish desires.

As social entrepreneurs, we should be passionate about our business. We should look beyond the immediate profit we get from it in order to move our business to the level of impact.

MY TIME MY FUND

There is a usual saying that time is money, time is life. This is another crucial fund we have as entrepreneurs is our time. The amount of time we spend in our business also determines the level of growth.

The time we spend reading books on marketing, accounting, product branding etc. are not waste of time, they only help us in improving and polishing our ideas. Most entrepreneurs find it difficult investing their time in things that would add value to their ideas or their business.

The time we spend in reviewing, reorganizing and evaluating our blueprint also goes a long way to help our business. As entrepreneurs, we should endeavor not to be passive in the daily activities of our business but rather we should be active.

The way we spend our time determines our growth in life so also our growth in the business world. Let us invest every little second into enhancing the advancement of our businesses.

OTHER PEOPLE'S MONEY

This is a medium in which most large business owners or entrepreneurs use. It is the most effective money used in sustaining a business.

Other people's money involves an entrepreneur selling his or her ideas to individuals who agrees to put down a percentage of the running cost or capital. This does not remove the entrepreneur as the owner of the business but rather enhance the business.

In order to build a business that makes impact, every entrepreneur must be interested in selling the ideas of his company to people who key into the business and provide the finance necessary for implementing the ideas.

Other people's money is a fund-raising system that helps the entrepreneur see the business as a separate entity of its own, it creates accountability and growth in business.

Using other people's money to run a business helps entrepreneurs to produce large numbers of goods and services which enhances the profit of the company. In using other people's money, the entrepreneur is not bordered about how the business is financed but rather he coordinates the finances and channels it to the right places.

When social entrepreneurs adopt the use of other people's money, they give the investors percentages of the profit as interest on the money invested while he takes a percentage of the profit and plows back the rest into the business to enhance its growth.

One of the greatest challenges for entrepreneurs is finding the resources and capital to start their venture – even more so for social entrepreneurs. It helps to first understand the different types of financing that are available, including various sources of private sector financing or financing from non-governmental organizations. Only then can you assess which financing options best suit your Social Purpose Business.

The struggle many social entrepreneurs have is engaging private and public investors who generally lack experience with the unique risks, business models and markets presented by social ventures. Investors consider Social Purpose Business a riskier investment because it tends to be relatively complex, takes longer to scale and often tackles uncharted areas.

Social enterprises thrive on investments, just like any other business. We have identified five types of investors interested in investing in social enterprises. Below we briefly outline the main characteristics of each type.

1. **Angel investor:** these investors invest in an organization based on ideological considerations. This means that the social mission of the investment target is the primary objective. Angel investors

focus strongly on social return before financial return. They often provide financial aid to start-ups and the amount of capital invested is relatively small, which means the risk for the angel investor is low.

The capital can be a one-time financial injection or ongoing support to carry the company through difficult times (e.g. the start-up period). Angel investors may be among the social entrepreneur's family and friends but can also be established foundations.

2. **Crowd funding:** crowd funders make use of platforms that bring together small amounts of capital from a large group of individuals. These individuals work together because they believe in the social mission and/or business model of a social enterprise. Depending on the group of people that participate, the focus can be on the social mission or the financial possibilities (in fact, this may differ per individual crowd funder).

To attract investors, crowdfunding makes use of the easy accessibility of vast networks of friends, family and colleagues through social media websites. As with angel investors, the amount invested per person is generally small, although the overall investment may be large.

3. **Financial institution:** these organizations have a significant sum of capital available and place more emphasis on financial return. The social mission is not necessarily the main business objective as is often the case with crowd funders and angel investors. While

financial institutions invest relatively large sums of money in social enterprises, they tend to choose less risky investments than venture capitalists.

4. **Investment fund:** this investor has a large, often conservative, amount of capital available. Investment funds aim to ensure steady growth in capital over the long term. Think for example of a pension fund—although stakeholders appreciate socially responsible investments, they are also interested in the long-term financial returns. Due to its future payment obligation, investment funds, such as pension funds, focus more on financial return than on social return and look for low risk investments.

5. **Venture capitalist:** this investor invests a large sum of money in start-up firms and small businesses with expected long-term growth potential. The risk for investors is high, but investments have potentially high returns (both social as well as financial).

The 'million-dollar question' is how the above observations can help social entrepreneurs to improve their access to funding. Based on our discussions and observations we formulated 4 guiding principles for social entrepreneurs when trying to get access to capital. Having an in-depth understanding of the business increases your chances of finding the right investor for the purpose of the enterprise. Focus and a clear vision of the purpose of the social enterprise can result in optimal impact for both parties.

1. Trade-offs do not exist! Alignment between financial and social objectives is key According to popular belief it is impossible to 'do good' and make a profit at the same time. However, the investors we interviewed tell a different story: profit (or a solid financial base) and impact can and should both play a prominent role. As a representative of a financial institution puts it: 'We expect that the social enterprise shows a convincing (social) mission, but also a convincing business case.' When integrated, the two aspects strengthen each other, making an attractive financial return to expand your impact.

Increasing the effect of your social mission can increase financial gain and vice versa. Investors look for organizations in which both aspects come together in an integrated way. For instance, angel investors might invest in idealists and look for ways to improve the entrepreneurial side of the social enterprise, while investment funds often start working with social entrepreneurs by focusing more on the entrepreneurial/financial side and assisting them with integrating their social goals.

A social enterprise integrates both the social mission and the financial drive to maximize its impact. Any suggestion that there might be a trade-off between the social and financial goals will weaken the business case. Investors not only expect you to have a clear understanding of your social goals and your business model, but they must be able to observe the integrated approach and vision. Most business cases that investors receive don't have a firm basis for making investment decisions. Be prepared to discuss and optimize your plan together with your investor.

2. Build and present a well-balanced management team. An investor will never believe that you make it on your own. Investors stress the importance of a team that shows its commitment to the social enterprise, rather than a single person. Having a group of people willing to invest time and effort in the social enterprise is regarded as an indicator of future success. Investors look for a social enterprise with a strong (management) team that shows a balance of complementary skills. Financial institutions, investment funds and venture capital firms specifically mention that they look for these signs when considering an investment.

Yet, this does not mean it is impossible to get funding on your own. Crowdfunding and angel investors, for instance, do support individuals, but in general investors are more likely to invest in a team. So, it is advisable to consider the inclusion of more people at an early stage. Gathering a management team in the organization that consists of a diverse group of people is preferred by investors. Apart from finding a suitable investor, it may strengthen your own organization as well. As one investor puts it: "Having more than one person gathered behind a leader or an idea shows persuasiveness and is a good indication that customers might follow."

3. Measure your impact! Your contribution becomes visible if measured Social enterprises find it difficult to measure their impact or at least quantify their outcome. Investors remarked that social enterprises often express that a lack of resources is one of the reasons for this. While not all investors set impact measurement as a minimum requirement before investing, all the investors that were interviewed indicated that it does make a stronger case. Financial institutions and venture capital firms expect the social enterprise they invest in to measure and quantify their impact.

Other investors also look for ways to measure impact but place less emphasis on it. All investors recognize the difficulty in measuring impact from their mission statement and at the same time acknowledge the value. "We see that it helps social entrepreneurs to bring focus to their work and identify more clearly what their goals are." The way social enterprises measure impact depends, among other things, on the maturity of the organization.

Starting organizations may for example find enough comfort in qualitative indicators, while the more experienced entrepreneur will often look for quantitative impact measurement. There is no consistency between investors with regard to what they ask and how they want to measure impact, but every investor is looking for ways to improve the effectiveness of the social enterprise by assessing the impact. The question remains how to get started. To prevent early dissolution, start with something small, easy to measure, preferably already available in your daily business. An example would be to measure the number of people you employ or the amount of positive feedback you receive. Every method has its limitations and there is no perfect system, but it allows you to see the progress you make and it brings focus to your work. Taking the question 'why' you want to measure your impact as a starting point will contribute to your alignment of financial and social objectives.

4. Avoid mission drift at all times! Mission drift occurs when an enterprise moves away from its initial mission.

This usually takes place after a couple of years, for example with new employees, leaders, owners or when a new investor is interested. Investors see mission drift as an issue when the focus of the social enterprise shifts from a balanced view towards financial gain, at the expense of the social mission. If mission drift occurs to the extent that the pursuit of financial gain no longer contributes to the pursuit of social gain, the mission may no longer be in line with what was initially discussed with the investor. Investors are therefore hesitant to commit themselves to long term investments. In theory, mission drift can also take place from a strong financial focus towards a more idealistic one. However, this rarely occurs with regard to young social enterprises.

Moving away from the initial mission is not necessarily a negative development. It depends on the expectations you and your investor(s) have. If you move more to financial gain, for instance, it is important that you are on the same page as your investors. Communicating expectations is the key message. Investors indicate that they find it increasingly important to discuss mission drift at the start of the investment. This is because they see mission drift occur around them. Aligning expectations and creating safeguards on this topic is important to prevent confusion and tension in the future.

Furthermore, starting the discussion with your investor on this topic shows that you have thought about how you can run your business in a sustainable manner. If you come to the conclusion that you want to prevent mission drift, there are different steps you can take. For example, you can include mitigating activities in the business plan, include legal entities or set up a supervisory board.

DEVELOPING A CULTURE OF MEASUREMENT

"My advice would be to measure, measure, and measure. Obviously, a final deep dive is critical for any campaign but to measure throughout the process, to be able to optimize your campaign in real time, is really important."

~ J Mawaka

To know if you are making progress or not in business, you need to have ways of measuring and monitoring your success.

TAKE INVENTORIES

As entrepreneurs, it is most important that we are accountable, not only in the aspect of finances but also in the sequence of event.

It is necessary to take note of daily events that occurs in the business front, it is important to take note of daily achievements, challenges that we come across in the business. These records are useful for further evaluations.

Taking notes of daily achievements help the business, the entrepreneurs and employee know that they are one step ahead, it also encourages the team to do more and put in their effort in improving the business.

Taking notes of daily challenges, helps the business or the entrepreneurs in knowing the likely challenges that the business faces on an average, it also helps improve the business, creating lasting solutions, it also serves as a way forward in relating with the challenges if it likely surface in the future. Where there are no records of likely challenges, although the business had faced a challenge before and come through it, it might be a stumbling block in the future if it ever comes again.

MANAGEMENT EVALUATION

The seat of management determines what happens in a company. It is very important to take inventories and also evaluate the growth of the management.

Poor management brings a fall to the business, while growth is the result of good management. It is important for entrepreneurs to always evaluate this management skill, the way he coordinates the staff, the way the production is made and the responds of clients to goods and services produced.

It is important that a good management works by the blueprint of the company, therefore the management should make it a point of duty to evaluate their walk with the blueprint. The progress they make, the stage they have got to, through the help of the blueprint.

It is important that the management evaluates their administrative role by seeking to know the opinion of their employees on how the management can further enhance the productivity and effectiveness of workers which may bring growth to the social enterprise.

EMPLOYEE EVALUATION

It is very important to evaluate the effectiveness of the employee, what are the things that enhance the effectiveness of these employees and what are the things that brings it down.

Employee surveys are very important in the growth of a business; these often help the entrepreneurs discover why the top performers in the team are performing well and why the underachievers are doing less than their best.

The attitude of employee to work are very important to know the belief they carry about the business. In building a strong team it is very important to have people who have like minds so that together they build the business.

Employee's reward is also important, in other to encourage the employee the entrepreneur could set up bonuses for hardworking employees, little assistance like soft loans, health care services could also be set in place. These rewards help encourage employees to put their best into work.

CUSTOMER EVALUATION

There are different types of people, as well as there are different types of products. It is important to evaluate the kinds of customers we have and why they are patronizing our businesses.

In order to be at an advantage in the business world, entrepreneurs must build good and solid customer relations.

Customer rewards and bonuses helps encourage customers to patronize our products more, it also gives room for new customers patronage. Customer opinion also matters, clients love to patronize business that would listen to their opinion and also work on it to improve their goods and services.

MEASURABLE GOALS AND
PRAGMATIC METRICS

In order to measure our success, we must have measurable goals and pragmatic and precise metrics by which we can assess our advancement toward the goals.

That's why the profit and loss statement is effective. Every business person can read it and understand the progress – or lack of it. The goal is clear and quantifiable: have more profit than loss. The P&L statement is a pragmatic and precise metric that shows whether that goal has been achieved or not.

The same two elements are true for measuring the success of the other strands of the triple bottom line. We must begin with figuring out what we are measuring – what are the specific, measurable goals we are hoping to achieve? Then we must figure out how we can measure it – what metrics will tell us if we are successfully reaching our goals?

BEGIN BY SETTING MEASURABLE GOALS

Every social entrepreneur has at least a foggy idea of why he is starting his business. They know they exist to solve a certain problem or make a certain impact. Yet an astonishing number of social entrepreneurs don't have concrete, quantifiable goals. As the fog becomes concretized, measurement is possible.

Sometimes that is easier said than done, but it is important that it be done at the outset. There is no way to know if you are accomplishing something if you don't know what you want to accomplish – duh! It is hard work – but it is the necessary starting point.

When setting measurable goals, start by identifying the social problem you wish to solve. Then begin broadly with your big picture goals and move toward the specific until you've identified goals you can actually measure. For instance, perhaps your business exists to help reduce poverty in a particular region. You want to create jobs as a way to reduce poverty. You could develop several specific goals out of this: create x number of jobs in the next year, provide job training to x number of people; reduce the unemployment rate by x percent, etc.

DEFINE PRAGMATIC METRICS

Once your measurable goals have been set, you need a way to track your progress on those goals. Sometimes this is very simple – such as quantifying the number of jobs you have created or using the local unemployment rate as a metric for the difference your business has or hasn't made. Other times you may have to get more creative – metrics for measuring social and spiritual transformation are not as clearly quantifiable.

Ultimately, social enterprise is about real people with real stories. Therefore, the stories of transformation of those your business has impacted are just as vital success indicators as numbers on a page. When a father in your community tells of how the job you have provided him has saved his children from the hands of traffickers, you know your business has made a real difference. His story is now a metric of your business's success in achieving one of its goals.

To determine if our social enterprise is achieving true triple bottom line success, we need to clearly identify the problem and figure out if we are making progress in solving it – whether it be poverty, corruption, human trafficking or otherwise. That starts with setting short, intermediate and long-term goals related to human change. Then we must define the metrics that will be used to measure the progress of these goals.

Only when we have set measurable goals and defined pragmatic metrics can we truly answer the question, "are we achieving success? Are we accomplishing what we set out to accomplish?"

MAKE MISTAKES

"Have no fear of perfection - you'll never reach it."

~ Salvador Dalí

Everyone at one point or another makes mistakes, mistakes are not bad in themselves but the way we view mistakes is what is important.

Mistakes are indicators that we did something. It indicates that we took actions which makes us far better than a person who didn't take action.

The famous entrepreneurs are made through the mistakes they made, using the lessons they learnt from their mistakes helps them become better entrepreneurs. Most times, we do not like to make mistakes, we feel hurt that we have done the wrong thing, but the solution is not to stay down. It is to review the actions we have taken and learn crucial lessons from the mistakes we make as entrepreneurs.

DROP THE BLAME

Many social entrepreneurs rather than accept that they have made a mistake, learn the lesson and apply the lessons learnt in other related aspect of the business sit back and beat themselves emotionally for the mistakes they have made. This is a very wrong way to treat mistakes. It does not allow us to pick the lessons in the situation and this may lead to reoccurring mistake.

Until we learn to take mistakes as part of life's way of teaching us to be better people and better entrepreneurs we may not be able to overcome the challenges that result from wrong choices.

As social entrepreneurs, it's slightly different because we're often looking to change markets rather than just enter them. We may even be aiming to create entirely new markets that don't yet exist.

The fact that our starting position as social entrepreneurs is slightly different to those of conventional business people can sometimes allow us to believe it's completely different – with the result being that we avoid asking ourselves important questions because we know we're not going to like the answers.

The big danger is that, because as social entrepreneurs, we understand what we're doing and why it's useful, we assume that other people will automatically understand that too and rush to engage with what we're doing without us do the hard work of convincing them that they should. They won't.

PART TWO

SOCIAL IMPACT

"Never doubt that a small group of thoughtful, committed, citizens can change the world. Indeed, it is the only thing that ever has."

~Margaret Mead

INTRODUCTION

In life, we all want to affect our lives and the lives of others around us, we all try to make impact in our society. A student who tries to study hard, bring home good grades and be good in his choice of career is aiming towards a goal. An armed robber who causes trouble, forcefully taking other people's belongings is also trying to make an impact. The difference between these two people and the impact they make is their driving force. The student has been driven by a positive force while the armed robber is being driving by a negative force.

Our driving force goes a long way to affect the kind of impact we make, when our driving force is positive we solve problems, we help our society become a better place to live in but if our driving force is negative we cause more havoc to the society and we become a source of terror to the people.

As an entrepreneur, we all want to make positive impact, we want to be known to have solved problems and enhance the society positively. In this section we would be looking at the things that would help enhance our business to make positive social impacts.

· What is social impact?

· Ways to make a social impact in your business.

· How to measure your social impact.

WHAT IS SOCIAL IMPACT?

According to Center for Social Impact (CSI) "Social Impact can be defined as the net effect of an activity on the community and the wellbeing of individual and family".

Social impact can be enhanced when business and individuals plan organizational focus and strategy to facilitate the rapid generation of successful and lasting solutions to different social problems.

There are different social problems which needs attention and the government cannot single-handedly solve all of them. They need the support of individuals and social enterprises to help solve these problems. Some of them include poverty, domestic violence, and unequal access to health care and poor educational facility.

As entrepreneurs who want to make social impact in our businesses, we can choose to support the government by making effort to improve the society in our little way. We should make impact the first focus of our businesses before the profit we make. A business focused on holding value to the society is indirectly adding value to itself and at the same time makes profit.

The level of impact we displayed is determined by our drive as individuals and also as entrepreneurs.

Your Drive

As individuals, we do not just act, our actions are controlled by our beliefs and our beliefs are accumulations of individual knowledge we have acquired over the years.

Humans are driven by either pains or pleasure, we do things that we associate pleasure with and try to avoid things we associate pains to.

If we learn to associate pleasure to making impact that is creating lasting solutions to social problems and also associate pains to seeing humans like us suffer, we would find adding values to the society easy and the world would be a better place to live in.

As we delight the growth of our businesses, in order to make impact in the business world we must also be able to discern what drives our actions in our businesses.

In the business world, entrepreneurs are driven by two things: profit and sacrifice. Although, the sole aim of every business owner is to make profit, some entrepreneurs are so profit conscious that they do not mind offering less quality goods and services to their clients so as to maximize the need to be satisfied in society, they put in their best and try to solve these needs in their own way and at the long run they make profit while trying to help in the society.

START WHERE YOU ARE

It is important to affect the society positively; these impacts can be achieved with the little resources we have; not necessarily money.

Many entrepreneurs believe that they do not make impact until they are able to develop a social development project for the society such as building of schools, pipe borne water etc. these are good visions, but this is not all to being a person of impact and building a business of impact.

Our employees, clients and investors are part of the society, the impact we want to add to the society can start from within. Some of our employees put in their best in our businesses; they help promote the business to another level, convincing clients that our products are the best they could get. These employees at one point or the other are not well to do, many of them needs us to encourage them and support their visions too.

When as entrepreneurs, we learn to support the visions of our employees; we are also adding value to the society. There are several ways we could support our employees, we can provide health facilities for them and also, we can help provide soft loans which they can have access to in order to help support them and we create conducive scheme for them to pay back.

Many entrepreneurs consider social impact as giving large donations to the society in order to support the social works. This is part of it, but it is not all there is about social impacts, in order to make impact in the society, we have to start from within our businesses.

The employees in our businesses are part of the society too, this is the best way to start making impact in our businesses, the impact we make in the lives of our employees, clients and investors speaks for us in public.

Social impact is not about picking a set of people we want to associate with and neglecting the others, the society is comprised of every family and individuals living in it, as entrepreneurs if we give large donations as a charitable act to the public and our employees do not benefit from these act within the business, all we are doing is nothing but a show off. Charity begins at home and this has to start from within the company.

Social impact is not all about giving donations to the society, when we minimize the negative consequences of our production is also part of making social impact. For example, when we run engines that does make noise, we abuse the social right of other individuals in the society but building a noise absolving plant also helps in reducing noise pollution in the society. This way we have also impacted the society.

UNDERSTAND YOUR AREA OF IMPACT

There are different areas where we could affect our society; these are so vast that as entrepreneurs, we cannot single-handedly cover all the areas.

We need to make survey of likely areas that have a

pressing need for attention in the society, taking a survey helps us to understand why those areas are most pressing in the society. It also helps us to understand how to attack problems in order to create long lasting solutions to these areas.

CREATE A SOCIAL GOAL

As entrepreneurs, it is important to create attainable social goals, we should not try to impact the society at the expense of our business and at the same time we should balance this with what we give.

As growing businesses, we should not invest in social donations that would at the long run affect our businesses; social donations are to be done from profits acquired from our businesses and not the running costs of the business.

It is very essential to save towards social donations this way; the business is not affected and at the same time the society benefits from it. For example, if we want to create a pipe borne water system for the community we are located we should first ask ourselves if that is the pressing need of the community and then count our cost save towards the project, when we do this, we do not deep into the business running cost, our employees and investors still get their benefit and at the same time the project is run and completed faster.

OFFER YOUR TIME

Sometimes it is not enough to give gifts, in the society we must learn to offer our time. The time we give also goes a long way to help the society. Sometimes, the society organizes days to clean up our environment; it is advisable to make out time to participate in these activities.

There are also places and people in the society where the best way to show that we truly care about them is going to pay them visit, encouraging them, this way we impact them with love and affection. For example, visiting the orphanage homes, prisons etc., when we make out time to do these things we also create impacts in the society.

There are times when our time is needed that the money we give or would like to give, there are times whereas entrepreneurs all the society needs from you is to give quality time, at these times the money we want to give might not meet the need of the society.

In our society today, there are also many less privileged children and youths who would love to be better but there is nobody to support them. These children and youth when they do not get encouragement, some of them drop their dreams being swayed by wrong association and become problems to the society by indulging in drugs and other criminal activities.

As entrepreneurs, one of the ways to support or impact the society is to encourage theses talents; there is a saying that the children and youths are the leaders of tomorrow and the strengths of the society. When we invest in the lives of these youths and children, we build the future of our society.

When we support talents, we support the society, these talented individuals when established still come back to impact the society remembering that their lives were built up by the society, they reciprocate the good deeds they benefited from social impact and that way the

chain of social impact is built in the society.

TEAM UP WITH LIKE MINDS

In our society, there are several business owners who are involved in social works, they whole-heartedly encourage and support the society with their incomes. As entrepreneurs, we should learn to work hand in hand with other people of like minds, this would help encourage us in doing more of the good works and collective yields more results.

When we team up with other businesses who have impact as their watch words, we grow the community, we make visible impact collectively and by doing this we also get support from each other.

There is a saying that two good heads are better than one, we as business owners come together and see to the needs of the society, it helps meet the needs of the society without each of the businesses been weighed down by expenses they still make significant impacts in the society.

WAYS TO MAKE A SOCIAL IMPACT IN YOUR BUSINESS

Every social enterprise's sole aim is to have an impact on the society.

We have set goals on how we want to impact our society and have also been working by these goals.

It is very important as entrepreneurs to make out time to measure what we have made in our businesses and to our environment.

You can't fake a mission based on social good.

When I think about startups that incorporate social good, I think about businesses that are always doing the right thing – for their team, for their community, for their customers, and for the environment. Most importantly, the decisions that they make naturally consider their social impact. They don't fake it and it is not a fad strategy – it is core to the business model. Social good isn't about doing something to just get attention.

Clearly Define and Communicate Your Social Impact!

Think through whether the fundamental problem your company solves is actually "social good." If so – define how. What is the social impact of the work you're doing? If successful, what is the social impact your company will have? Your team has to believe it in order for them to execute, and in order for them to share the impact they're having in the community and with your customers. Is it a leap? Or is it real?

MAKE IT PART OF YOUR COMPANY'S

CULTURE

As an entrepreneur, you have to communicate your social impact clearly with your team early and often before you can make the case for doing it externally. It has to be ingrained in everything you do. And it must naturally connect to your business' mission and vision.

BE AUTHENTIC ABOUT YOUR

IMPACT

Don't create a social good strategy solely to generate revenue. It won't work because people will see through it. Rather, connect the dots internally and externally on how your company can make a positive social impact throughout your business model. And if you can't, don't force it.

If your company's mission isn't to change the world, that's okay too – there are other ways to incorporate social good into your model. For example, some employers choose to empower their employees to use paid time off to donate to the charity of their choice.

Integrating social impact into your business model shouldn't be an afterthought and it shouldn't be temporary. It should be central to achieving your vision.

Otherwise, it might just be a distraction — one that your clients and employees will see through.

Most business owners hope to make a positive difference in the world. To varying degrees, many of them do. However, the drive to build a company that has a direct social impact has led to it becoming a loaded term where not all social enterprises are created equal.

Generally speaking, a social enterprise is one that puts business tools to use in meeting a social need. This could be bringing technologies to remote regions of the world or reducing waste while helping people in need. A social enterprise can overlap with social innovation, which is a term that describes a business finding innovative ways to address social needs.

However, a business doesn't have to be community service-oriented to make a difference in the world. In fact, the global economy has reached a tipping point where emerging markets are now taking center stage, with every business now having the potential to seriously impact society. This goes beyond charitable organizations to include businesses of all sizes in banking, mobile communications, utilities, and more.

Whether through the services they deliver, their employment practices, or through their other activities, today's businesses have an impact on society. Here are a few examples of how various types of companies enact social change in the work they do.

TRADITIONAL NONPROFITS

By their very definition, non-profits exist to provide a service without making a profit. Any money these organizations make must be reinvested into the cost of furthering their mission. One example of a nonprofit social enterprise is the March of Dimes, which puts resources toward preventing premature births. This organization has a history dating back to 1938, but like many other nonprofits, it continues to make a difference across the world with the work its employees do, saving the healthcare system an estimated $70 billion or more by 2020.

MISSION-FIRST BUSINESSES

Unlike most businesses, mission-first companies are oriented around a socially impactful mission but operate as a for-profit enterprise. Although they generate revenue, the emphasis is always on making change. In this model, growth is a means to making a larger impact. The ability to interweave profit with impact helps these businesses grow, innovate, and take risks, which are all components of very successful companies overall.

Be a Socially Responsible Business

Socially responsible businesses may not put social impact first, but they realize the many benefits of being community minded. By operating with a conscience, they show their concern for the environment, as well as the health of the community where they are located.

Patagonia is an example of a business that emphasizes the importance of social responsibility as an add-on to the work it does. As a result, the company sets the tone as an environmentally-conscious organization that cares about its customers and the future of the planet as a whole. This provides brand exposure without constant product marketing.

BIG DONORS

Instead of sending a social message, large corporations can opt to put their effort behind financial contributions. Many large companies make charities a part of their annual activities, both for the positive impact it makes and the tax deduction they receive for it. Salesforce has adopted a 1-1-1 philosophy, which has the company donating one percent of its earnings, one percent of its products, and one percent of employee time to various charitable causes it supports. Considering Salesforce has a $73 billion market cap, the math demonstrates that this donation makes a serious difference in the world. The corporation focuses its own efforts on education, with grants that go directly to the very communities where its employees live and work.

Social impact initiatives are also evolving as organizations realize they don't have to choose just one way to engage in community-minded activities. They can employ a blend of the above methods that better meet their mission and help them further their brand reputation.

HOW TO MEASURE SOCIAL IMPACT

As a social enterprise, the sole aim is to impact our society positively. These impacts should be measured per time. It is important to measure our impact on the society, our clients, staffs and investors. This helps us to know our level of progress and also helps view ourselves in the eye of the public.

It is also very important to measure our impact in order to be sure that the area of impact we have chosen is of high value to the society, if the area of our impact is of little value to the society although we put our best to get the work done, we have the passion to see things change in this aspect, it would bring little or no yield because the society does not see that aspect as of economic value.

For a social enterprise it is essential to be able to measure social impact, after all the measurement of social impact is a direct correlation to answering the question 'What does your enterprise do?' For a social enterprise, answering that question must go beyond simply achieving a respectable profit margin, as a social enterprise, our social or environmental impact is how we show the value of our organisation.

There are many reasons why you should be measuring

your social impact; measuring social impact allows you to manage it which is critical for organisations wanting to improve and of course expand your impact. Whether you want to scale, raise investment or even win contacts, by measuring your social impact you can provide critical data which will help achieve these improvements and expansions to your business. In an ever increasingly competitive market for social enterprises those who are able to successfully measure their social impact are better placed to attract further capital to continue their positive changes to society.

Embedding the way in which you measure impact into your enterprise from the beginning will allow you to keep on top of it and continually use results to build upon and improve.

So how does a social enterprise actually measure social impact? There unfortunately isn't a simple answer to this that can be applied to all social enterprises. You have to consider the size of your enterprise, what stage it is at and the mission and goals of your enterprise.

For a small startup social enterprise a common-sense approach to measuring social impact can go a long way. This means there is no need to spend money on bringing in external evaluators or get bogged down in rigorous and complex models of impact measurement. For a small company, the best way to measure social impact is to answer these basic questions, what is the mission of my enterprise? how many people have I reached? If your goals are environmental track the geography and measure the size of the areas that you have reached, the number of people who have benefited from your organisation. Comparing these numbers with the overall goals of your enterprise will give a basic idea of where your company is at and if it is achieving interim goals you should have set. Measuring social impact is just as important for keeping on target for monthly goals or yearly goals it is not just about measuring against the end goal of the enterprise.

For small enterprises, at the beginning of their journey, measuring social impact is still of vital importance, so it is important to discuss ways in which you could use a common-sense approach to justify your social impact to external parties such as prospective investors or the community in which you have set up. One way of doing this could be to use a case study to demonstrate your impact. Choose perhaps one individual you have succeeded in helping, provide information of their circumstances before your intervention, what changes you made to their life, focusing specifically on how your programme brought about the changes, reminding your audience that were it not for your enterprise being available then the life of this person would not have achieved such a positive change. This case study can include videos, quotes, podcasts etc., as well as including cold hard facts; we are talking about social change, so it is important it has heart as well.

It important to remember that measuring social impact is not a process in which you must feel you are defending your enterprise, it is a valuable tool to help progress internally as well externally to your enterprise. What you learn from the assessment will be able to positively inform any strategy or operational changes to your organisation. Hence it is important to go into the process as open minded as possible. Evaluation needs to be built in to the way you work and not a standalone process.

As your enterprise grows and data collection and analysis grows more complex, this is where employing a more rigorous system for measuring social impact becomes important. There are two main systems for measuring social impact; Social Audit Network (SAN) and Social Return on Investment (SROI).

A social audit is an external assessment of the process for social accounting. The process for social accounting has four main stages as illustrated in the image below:

First phase: Social Enterprise:

* Identifying the social enterprise's vision, mission and values
* Setting objectives and priorities to meet the vision
* Defining the long-term vision and what the social enterprise will achieve in the long-term
* Outlining the medium-term strategy and the key milestones
* Laying down the short-term operational criteria

Second phase: External View:

* Assessment of stakeholders and services delivered
* Evaluation of benefits received by external stakeholders
* Identification of problems
* Design, planning and implementation of solutions

Third phase: Internal View:

* Assessment of the organisation
* Evaluation of the effectiveness of operations
* Review of the efficiency of the management systems
* Appraisal of the board members, staff and volunteers' satisfaction

Fourth phase: Review and Planning:

* Learning lessons
* Making changes for improvements
* Planning the following year's strategy and criteria

The above process is an effective way of monitoring performance, it allows stakeholders to have a say and is effective in having the ability to highlight areas in which improvements can be made, unfortunately it is not without its drawbacks, it is a time consuming process and you have to factor in the cost of social auditors, hence why this method is not recommended for small startup enterprises as they could well be costs that you are not at a stage you can afford. There is also the danger of manipulating stakeholder views, but if you have taken on board the advice of previous articles then you should have stakeholders that you trust implicitly to be honest and professional.

The other method, SROI, measures service outcomes to compare the financial investments made against the benefits created for the stakeholders (added value).

A longer-term assessment of the value of outcomes in terms of market values or values to government or other 'proxies' and putting a sterling value on them. The term proxy is a substitute source of the value of the outcomes but must be a reliable source for example the EU.

Below is a template of an impact map:

Impact map

Stakeholders	Inputs	Outputs	Outcomes	Impacts
	Value of contract	Description of service contracted to deliver	Additional outcomes	Proxy value of each additional outcome and calculation to support statement

Once again, we must weigh up the pros and cons of the above method, an advantage of this method is that it is much less time consuming, its step by step process makes it easy to follow and the way in which the data is encapsulated makes it very useful in terms of marketing and selling.

The use of proxies however is where the disadvantages come in; there is an obvious danger of using them to overstate values. Also, as a social enterprise you will inevitable have a lot of 'soft outcomes' such as 'quality of life' it can be very difficult to find a proxy from a reliable source that is able to put a value on that. One potential way of measuring soft outcomes could be to use both subjective self-reporting – a 5-point scale – and objective indicators; activities that confidence might produce. Using these measures to assess your service users at strategic intervals such as before, at the end and some months after will enable you to gain further insight into your social impact.

It should be noted that if your enterprise is in a position to hire an external SROI technician to carry out the assessment, then you need to ensure that they are accredited, since it is a relatively new sector there are many 'cowboys' out there who follow unofficial templates and provide reports with inflated results which may look pleasing but will do harm in the long run and this also undermines the credibility of the method.

Having looked at a few different methods of measuring social impact, we also need to remember that measuring social impact needs to remain an enabling process, Jonathan Coburg; Director of Social Value Lab sums it up as:

"Impact measurement is designed to help understand and strengthen social impact. When impact measurement begins to dominate the discussion rather than impact creation, there is a danger we will lose sight of our goals. It is not helpful when the tools to measure social impact organisations to become side-tracked or to allocate a disproportionate amount of time."

Whilst there is no one method of measurement there is a well-developed approach for building your measurement framework; this was developed by the NPC (New Philanthropy Capital) – a think tank and consultancy for charitable organisations. It is called the

Four Pillar Approach and is summarized in the image below:

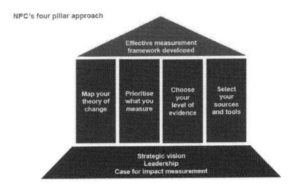

NPC's four pillar approach

This approach whilst not the only one available is suitable for all levels of social enterprise so I believe is a good one to include.

Looking more closely at the four steps;

Step One: Map your theory of change – this map shows what you want to achieve as an organisation and how you plan on achieving it, as a map it will set out the causal links between your activities and the goals you have set in place. This framework is what will underpin your measurement efforts.

Step Two: Prioritize what you will measure – This is why it was important to have a clear definition of social impact; the impacts of your enterprise will affect different people and sectors in different ways hence it is important to know which outcomes are of greatest importance to measurement of social impact. It's also important to include data on possible negative consequences of your work, so when it comes to prioritizing whilst it might be tempting to put negativity lower on the list, knowing what you're doing wrong or not well provides vital information for improvement, so it is still a high priority.

Step Three: Choose your level of evidence – The different approaches discussed in this chapter provide some examples of ways in which you can choose your level of evidence dependent upon what is best for your enterprise based on its current status and level of development.

Step Four: Select your sources and tools – So dependent on the approach you have chosen in the above step you can select which sources and tools most suit your level of evidence.

The full NPC guide is freely available to download and is a good resource for those starting enterprises and looking to develop a template on ways to measure their impact.

Finally, it is important to remember that the measurement of social impact needs to remain a means to an end rather than an end in itself. The process of measurement needs to be built into everyday business therefore it needs to remain manageable; this is where the importance of selecting the right method of impact measurement for your Enterprise comes in. Just because one method is more expensive than another does not make it a better method, there is no flag ship method or gold standard method, the needs and stage of the enterprise determine what type of method is correct for you, so do not focus on what methods other enterprises around you may be using but make sure you keep it manageable and choose what is best for your enterprise.

This chapter has given an overview of the ways in which social impact can be measured, however the most important thing to take away is just how increasingly important it is to measure social impact whether you are only starting out and are relying on internal members to measure the impact via common sense approach or if you are growing beyond that and are employing more statistical methods.

Measuring social impact is key for a social enterprise, to finish off here are a few reasons why:

- Access to finance
- Measuring impact is a sign of a well-run ship
- It helps tell your story to stakeholders
- Achieving your purpose

And most importantly impact reporting is here to

stay, if your enterprise is to succeed in this increasingly empirical world, then we need the proof. *"Show me the money"* will become *"show me the impact"*.

PART THREE

YOUR BRAND

"Your personal brand is a promise to your clients… a promise of quality, consistency, competency, and reliability"

~JASON HART

INTRODUCTION

A strong brand is always consistent: Communicating your brand needs to be consistent across all platforms, through all the employees, through your visual identity and through your values - this to me is the key to a successful, strong brand which people can relate to.

Be careful when involving customers and consumers in creating a brand: They should form an integral part of the research you do but creating a brand by committee could lead to a much-fractured approach - you can't please everyone and trying to do so could sacrifice some of the values of the brand. Experts identified within the organization should consult and research the needs, wants and opinions of the customers and then use this knowledge to establish the brand.

Develop your logo: Rather than worrying about choosing one design to stick with forever is more important to find a visual identity which accurately reflects the organization's values - it can be built on, tweaked and changed over time. Often, the simpler the better.

You need to back-up your brand with a good business model: I think the biggest problem with social enterprises is a lack of good long-term revenue-generating business models. I'd rather see a social enterprise with a good business model and a terrible brand, which can be fixed, than a well-branded social enterprise that does not have a good business model.

Involve your customers: Some of the key questions we've posed for our start-up social enterprises are about how they will reach their potential customers and differentiate themselves from competitors; the ongoing involvement of those customers in the development of the business can be part of the social mission and an important USP.

Ensure any associations are tightly aligned: Ensure the alliances you build are mutually beneficial. Within your marketing and business plan you should always know the direction in which you want to go and where you want to end up. If the social enterprise industry groups aren't offering this then don't go there: find someone and build alliances with people that can take you in the right direction.

A brand should uphold the whole ethos of your social enterprise: A true brand is the face of your business; it should uphold everything that your business stands for and that is why it is so important to ensure your brand is protected and marketed/communicated to your potential consumers/market correctly.

Let your brand develop with your business: Until you start building your business, know what you want to do and are trying to achieve, any new business will go through multiple reiterations until they come up with a winning formula. It is at this point for me that the time is right to start thinking about building your brand.

The social enterprise marketplace should be treated as you would any other: The social enterprise marketplace should not be any different to any other marketplace that does B2B or B2C. Social enterprises are able to communicate part of their brand value as working for social benefits - this gives them an advantage, but they are still associations within their own right and need to be able to compete.

Don't rely on quality marks: There is a value in service and quality marks, but I do not think they offer as much clout toward consumers as they do in B2B conversations. We are in communication with teams that have filed for marks and are exploring the cumulative value. I am worried about low take-up of these kinds of quality awards and how a lack of auditing may dilute its potential value.

The social enterprise mark can be useful for start-ups: A social enterprise's own brand should come first, but it can be strengthened if it is associated with the social enterprise community, including the social enterprise mark. The mark is particularly important to start up social enterprises - it adds an instant credibility to your brand (as well as the other benefits).

Brand Evaluation is the first part of the process and involves research into, and an understanding of, internal and external perceptions of your proposition or current brand and the dynamics of your marketplace.

In the second part of the process, Brand Development, this information is used to help us create a range of possible brand positioning, personalities and values.

The third part, Brand Realization, is designed to demonstrate how the new brand might come to life more specifically; detailing all its brand attributes and brand elements.

The final Brand Implementation module involves applying the brand created to the design and production of all communications material to produce dynamic, coordinated and effective marketing collateral.

BRAND EVALUATION

The Brand Evaluation process is all about immersing yourselves in the marketplace in which your business operates, whilst also gaining a detailed understanding of your brand.

Put simply, its aim is primarily to help everyone involved in the 'Branding Project' to understand:

- the client their brand
- their products and services their market
- their competitors

This can be achieved by conducting an audit of the marketplace (both external and internal) to understand the key points of brand interaction. Information on brand values, history and the services the brand offers, would also be gathered and assessed.

By analyzing these market research findings you can start to define the dynamics of the marketplace, such as how much of a role personality plays within your specific market, the current success factors and key drivers for business within it and any key points of brand interaction.

Some of the key questions that you will require answers to in this module include:

What is the business objective? What is the marketing objective? What is the brand positioning? What is your overall proposition?

Do you have a genuine point of difference?

What do your staff and customers think about you?

How do your competitors' offers differ to yours?

What are the mandatories?

What is the big picture – real and perceived?

At the end of this Brand Evaluation process, you can start to clarify the brand values, services and position in the marketplace. Effectively 'The new brand position.'

You can then move on to the second part of the branding process.

BRAND DEVELOPMENT

The objective of this part of the process is to define the dynamics of the 'new brand' (and the marketplace) more specifically.

. In so doing you can develop the most effective verbal and visual branding route for you.

From the information gained in the Brand Evaluation part, the target audience, key messages and brand values can be defined. Success factors of competitors and insights into market attitudes can be considered and a visual articulation of the brand can be explored.

All options considered will explore a different way to visually articulate the 'New Brand Position.'

For example: Name*

Signature (logotype) Strapline Positioning

Core values

Colour palette

Typography Imagery

Tone of voice Graphic elements

At the end of this Brand Development stage, one definitive option will have been agreed upon and this will define your vision for your brand.

BRAND REALIZATION

In the Brand Realization part of the process, learnings from the Brand Evaluation section and the agreed brand option are realized in the form of working design principles and applied to specific marketing collateral such as shop fascia, website, brochure etc.

This helps to better:

- Understand the brand vision, brand assets and brand positioning

- Understand the marketing and sales vision, targets and requirements

- Understand customer requirements, perception and environment

- Exploit relevant brand values for agreed marketing strategy

- Realize creative solutions within a commercial framework

At this stage any issues concerning the application of the 'brand tools', brand values and tone of voice can be raised and resolved before final implementation is begun.

Implementation of the brand across these marketing materials will test the success of its application.

BRAND IMPLEMENTATION

With the brand positioning agreed and the design principles approved, the implementation of the full range of marketing collateral to support the brand can begin.

A synergy across all marketing collateral is key to a creating a cohesive brand. However, whilst this does not mean that everything should look the same, it does mean that wherever you touch the brand, the visual identity and tone of voice should be consistent and reiterate the new brand and its values.

Name Generation

Why are brand names important?

Brand names are important because, quite simply, first impressions count. They set up an expectation of what the brand will deliver, and whilst the products, packaging and retail environment might change, the name won't. So, if a new name is for life, you must be sure, to choose one you can live with, and the first step in making that choice is to define the role of the new name:

Is it going to sit with the existing market language? Or Be a radical departure from everything else in the marketplace?

Secondly, it is important to think about the type of name you require. For example, should it be:

Descriptive Evocative

Obviously the more abstract the name the more time and money may be required to build an understanding of the brand. The more descriptive the name, the more problems you are likely to have in creating stood out or registering the name at Companies House, as a Trademark or as a domain name online.

Should you create a brand name?

It would be good to be able to explain here the industry standard process for name generation, but the simple fact is there are no rules regarding where a name comes from, except to say it is largely perspiration with a hint of inspiration.

Here, though, is an example of some of the more familiar sources of 'perspiration':

- Family names
- Product ingredients
- Nature/Agriculture/Environment

- Greek/Roman Gods

- Foreign language

- Made up names

Obviously, a browse through the Thesaurus, papers and dictionaries is valuable too.

However, the best way to start the process is with a creative workshop, exploring as many words and phrases that you can think of that relate to your brand, your market and your audience. It is also worth remembering that to get the best from a workshop session everything is relevant, and nothing should be deemed wrong or inappropriate at this stage.

Bringing the brand name to life

When you are creating a new name, it will initially lack context when first seen and heard, unlike established brand names that immediately convey a style, promise, meaning and emotion that has been built up over time. So, you must try hard not to judge any proposed name in isolation and try instead to get a feel for your brand name and your offer.

There are several ways to do this.

1. Say it

I. The more you say a name the more comfortable you become with it.

'New name, New name, New name, New name.'

ii. Put it into the context of a sentence too.

'I've just bought some New name

product, it's terrific.'

'The great thing about New name

is their extensive product range?'

iii. Get different people to say it.

See how those familiar with the name and those seeing it for the first time say it. Try it with would- be customers and people of different ages and different regional accents. How do they pronounce it? Can they say it easily?

2. Visualize it

Think about how the name might look in the marketplace, on a pack or in store. These visual triggers will help your audience understand your brand name and brand offer better. This visual language will also help you get a clear understanding of how you are going to position your brand, as the example below demonstrates.

3. Support it

Depending on the name you choose a supporting or qualifying line may also be required to explain or define the brand name. This may be used initially and then changed or developed as the brand grows, or ultimately dropped as the brand name becomes well recognized in its own right. Either way the power of a supporting line should not be overlooked.

For example:

The future's bright. The future's xxxxxx

xxxxxx. Because you're worth

it. l. Every little helps.

THE CONTEMPORARY BRAND

The contemporary brand

- Traditional

- Contemporary

- Radical

BRANDING AND SOCIAL ENTERPRISE

When approaching brand work for a Social Enterprise, it is important never to make any differentiation or allowances just because of that fact. The issues facing such enterprises from a brand perspective are no different from those facing any commercial organization, in that they require the best solution at the most economically viable cost.

As demonstrated in this document, always attempt to think in a relevant fashion, relevant that is to the project in hand.

Working on branding projects for a Social Enterprise does, however, demand that one is aware and sensitive to the following:

- Any brand identity solution must not come with implications for expensive ongoing implementation.

• Just because it's a Social Enterprise does not mean that any creative solutions should look patronizing in any way or 'cheap' in execution.

• Just because it's a Social Enterprise does not mean that any creative solutions should focus on this as the solution itself.

Other key observations one would make with regard to how any Social Enterprise might approach a branding project from scratch are as follows:

• Forget that you are a Social Enterprise. Approach professional creative agencies to help you develop the brand. Your projects might carry much smaller budgets but the work itself is exciting and challenging, which matters as much to such people as the money

•Don't be tempted to use non- professional companies such as university departments either on a pro-bono or limited fee basis.

Branding is a complicated business and should not be trusted to amateurs, no matter how full of good intentions they are

• Get involved! Branding projects are unique in many respects in that it is your chance to really influence the 'brand' from the start. Once the brand identity is created all that follows, by the nature of it, must conform, so make the most of the development process

• Creatives hate a blank canvas so work hard on the brief. The work they deliver is only ever as good as the briefs they get, and the level of client involvement. You will always know more about your proposed brand than they can, particularly at the start. Tell them about your vision, share examples of work from similar or different organizations which you think they should see make them aware of any politics or other fundamental issues which might constrain their thinking or approach. The more you put in at the start, the more you will get out at the end.

• Creating brands obviously has legal implications, and thus costs! From the start you should factor in costs for legal fees, especially if a new brand name is being created. If you want to try to trademark your new brand this also comes at a cost.

Finally, enjoy the process if you can. Developing new brands or concepts is not a regular, daily activity, such projects really are rare in that nothing is set in stone and anything can be considered in arriving at the solution you desire. Once established the brand is real and everything that follows will come with constraints which were non-existent at the start.

SOCIAL MEDIA AND BRANDING FOR SOCIAL ENTERPRISES

Social media is one of the most underutilized tools for many startups. This can be one of your most valuable tools as the call to action (in this case purchase) can remain consistent long-term. It has the opportunity to unite a community against an issue. A social good brand is just that, social! Social brands have the highest form of brand loyalty. The consumer shares, posts. Photos became the essential ingredient in our growth" he also points out that "without these brand evangelists typing captions under their photos of how they fed 10 children in the Horn of Africa we would not have been able to change a million lives. No marketing is powerful than the word of mouth." And, nowadays word of mouth translates to personal social media handles.

PART FOUR

RUNNING YOUR SOCIAL ENTERPRISE

"You don't learn to walk by following rules. You learn by doing and falling over." ~Richard Branson

INTRODUCTION

Social enterprises are businesses that bring a lot of positive impact to their societies and are profitable while at it. In the day to day activities involved in the running and maintaining a business as a social enterprise, there are hitches and obstacles that might arise along the way.

It is important to realize what these obstacles might be, how to handle them in order to successfully run your social enterprise.

Also, since the social enterprise has a goal and a mission it wants to achieve, there are ways to measure your success and see if you are making progress or not.

LEARN TO HANDLE REJECTION

In our world, we understand that we will encounter rejection in our own lives as we build our own businesses. But when it happens, it is a different scenario. Whether it is a rejection or a significant bump in the road, it is extremely easy to get lost in the overwhelming sense of loss. Many of us do not even want to get started in our social ventures because we fear rejection, we do not want to be rejected.

One rejection may easily lead to times of dismissing commercial tasks and going after comfort-giving, pleasure-bringing activities such as watching your favourite TV series or binge-viewing your favoured Netflix series. If you take action to achieve your goals, one definite thing is that you would experience rejection constantly. If you are not, you must ask yourself whether you are taking big steps. Growing occurs whenever you step beyond your comfort zone to do the things which scare you.

Rejection is hard for anyone. When you're running a social enterprise or business and an entire team is dependent on your success, it's even more stressful. Entrepreneurs carry a heavy load. Rejection should not discourage you, nor should it end your dreams. If you pay attention, you'll find out that you'll actually succeed in spite of those rejections

So, how do I handle rejection in my social enterprise? You might ask. Here are the things to do whenever you encounter rejections so as to effectively handle rejection in your social enterprise.

DON'T MAKE IT TOO PERSONAL

Business people regularly tragically take rejection by and by. We as a whole have sentiments, all things considered. It's imperative to note, nonetheless, that on the grounds that your thought got shot down or your association was rejected as a social entrepreneur, it doesn't mean it's a reflection on you.

Try not to give rejections a chance to get to you. Rather, take a gander at the rejection for simply what it is: Was it an awful strategy for success? Would it be safe to say that it was the wrong association terms? Is it accurate to say that it was the wrong planning? Instead of pointing the finger at yourself, evaluate what the genuine purposes behind rejection were.

Huge numbers of my initial rejections would have made me bankrupt. Gratefully, I didn't give it a chance to get to me and I could conquer these minor difficulties with shockingly better results.

Take a minute to give your outrage a chance to be expressed

You're human even as a social entrepreneur. You can have a go at bundling every last one of those notions and sentiments inside anyway favourable circumstances with that framework. In the long run, you'll explode - undoubtedly in a situation that you regret. Allow your humankind to let out. Yell or leave control, go for a run, take it out on your punching pack.

Take some time and discuss with a trusted partner, so that you could be given some advice on the rejection you faced and how better to handle such a situation. You could also consult with a group of friends who are knowledgeable about the rejection. They will help you express your outrage and also help you see things from a clearer point of view.

LEARN FROM IT

Credit it to a staggering feeling of pride; however, business visionaries usually feel that they have the best opinion and viewpoint of things. They usually think that every other person is not so knowledgeable and can learn from them. While there might be some reality to that, it's critical to learn and seek the lesson from every rejection you face in your social enterprise. In the event that your product or item was rejected for a specific reason, investigate and check whether you can improve your unique thought.

I've made incredible changes and modifications to the services and products rendered by my company after facing a series of rejections. By focusing on criticism about what individuals extremely needed and what they're not keen on, we've possessed the capacity to tailor our solutions, products, and services to precisely what is needed by the clients. It's a win-win situation if you ask me. You are better, your product is better, your clients are satisfied.

DETERMINE YOUR NEXT MOVE

Your following stages after a rejection must be key and strategic. Take a couple of days to design out what to do straightaway. If it requires that you get more mastery, be particular about how to do that and connect a timetable to it. On the off chance that it's making an alternate way to deal with how you go after some opportunities, prioritize what opportunity to go after per time as a social entrepreneur.

USE IT TO FURTHER WEIGH YOUR ASPIRATIONS AS A SOCIAL ENTERPRISE

It takes a considerable level of thought and activity to start a social enterprise. There will be lots of time when you are simply not inspired to continue in your social enterprise. You might even be distressed and motivated to give up when facing series of rejections. There's a mindset shift that can give you the fuel you require to get inspired. Utilize every rejection as flame to light you up and spur you.

In life, you get involved in various forms of endeavors and exercises. Those exercises enable you to end up the best form of yourself. You can choose how to respond to the rejection, you can determine how you see the rejection. Get considerably more resolved to achieve that objective. Utilize the rejection as your inspiration to keep taking the necessary steps. Toward the day's end, taking every necessary step reliably is the thing that constructs your business and achieves your objectives - it's not your sentiments and feelings.

TEACH OTHERS

Regularly, the reason you get rejected, particularly in business, is on the grounds that you haven't taught your audience and other observers well enough. In reality as we know it, where there are such a large number of "disruptors," you need to realize that the world may not be very prepared for your product or services. Take worries that are raised and utilize them as a way to teach general society or your clients about your thought, business or arrangement.

In my office, we accumulate each rejection and utilize them as methods for instructing ourselves. We make an assortment of substance to address basic rejection letters and utilize it to potential prospects for what reason we're a decent accomplice.

In spite of the fact that as social entrepreneurs, we shouldn't consider rejection to be the apocalypse and particularly as something awful, there is something great that leaves each terrible circumstance. We'll talk about how to make rejection function for you and your business, and in addition adapting methodologies for business people.

REMIND YOURSELF THAT YOU'RE

SUPPORTED

It isn't everyone who will support you or your business brand. You have to see through a looking glass and pick those and surround yourself with those who will support you.

Dr. Winch suggests, in the wake of rejection, surround yourself with the people who do support you:

"Let's remind you of the people who value you, who love you, who enjoy you, who think you are fun. Reinstate that right away. As soon as possible. And that is a very important thing to do, in terms rejection."

DON'T BE ANXIOUS

Everybody detests rejection. Sam Stoves has made $10million in his profession, however needed to manage an immense dread of rejection in the first place. So, have numerous different representatives and ladies. You simply need to drive yourself. You'll most likely find after that first rejection; it isn't that awful. Being frightful will just make individuals accept you're unserious and it demonstrates you're simply not removed to be a social entrepreneur.

APPRECIATE THE WINS

(REGARDLESS OF HOW LITTLE)

In Composing, Stephen Lord clarifies that before distributing his breakout novel, his compositions were the casualty of a great many rejections, while his family was toeing the neediness line. Little wins—short stories bringing a couple of dollars from magazines—had a major effect in examination and urged him to continue composing.

"In the event that you composed something for which somebody sent you a check, on the off chance that you got the money for the check and it didn't bob, and on the off chance that you at that point paid the light bill with the cash, I think of you as capable." — Stephen Ruler

Hardship comparatively enabled Michael to see the thin silver coating that was the moderate development of Pack:

"Despite the fact that I continued getting turned as the month progressed, we were gaining ground. I was offering my auto, maximizing my MasterCard's, taking credits from family, my significant other was maintaining two sources of income, I was offering apparel, I was doing whatever it took. Be that as it may, my business was developing."

Despite the fact that I continued getting turned down as the month progressed, we were gaining ground.

REMAIN CENTERED

Lack of concern breeds average quality. Rejection advises us that we have space to develop, connects with the focused soul, and, when outfit, can give inspiration to continue.

REAFFIRM YOUR OBJECTIVES

Would you say you are still as energetic about your thought after rehashed rejections from financial specialists? Is it accurate to say that you are pushing forward with building your social enterprise, despite the fact that you still can't seem to make deals? Your answer will enable you to choose, Michael says, on the off chance that you should remain on track or shift gears.

LEARN HOW TO HANDLE FINANCIAL PRESSURE

No one needs to consider their business failing. Social entrepreneurs that don't have a plan much of the time fall back on the reason that they should be totally committed to their business, anyway that is poor basis. You can center on a business and still prepare to be financially unfaltering if that business goes under. Various great businessmen failed a couple of times already finding their tremendous triumphs.

A good plan truly empowers you to focus on your business impressively more, as it frees you up from struggling with what you will do if the business doesn't work out. Here are a few hints for how to set yourself up to survive the most critical result believable of your business going under:

1. Have a clear divide between Personal and Business Finances

There should be a mass of division between your own assets and the corporate record. This will ensure that you put aside additional money for yourself and don't lose everything on the business. Simply more basically, it shields you from being stuck in a difficult situation financially.

Your business should be a separate entity of its own. Or else, you risk paying any commitments the business procures out of your own pocket.

2. Keep Yourself Marketable

You may not plan to work for someone else until the end of time, yet it's up 'til now a brilliant idea to stay employable while building your own one of a kind business. Following your activity inside the association can help give potential organizations setting for what capacities and experience you may pass on to the table.

Online classes and accreditations are an exceptional technique to keep up with the most recent activities while on a tight timetable. These classes will tell supervisors you haven't fallen behind in your field while wearing down your business. Most will similarly be particularly enlivened by your responsibility in finding time to work in those classes.

3. Pay Yourself What You're Worth

Value your work in your company and pay yourself a legitimate pay for someone in that activity. Various businessmen will simply pay themselves the littlest they need to survive. Not only does it put your own assets at risk, it furthermore makes a beguiling photograph of your association's records.

Paying yourself a fitting salary gives you the resources for take care of principal expenses and put aside money. It moreover empowers you to factor in how much capital you should finance your social enterprise whole deal, and it saves you from certainly changing your cost structure two or three years apart.

It's best to have a great deal of money saved when starting another business so when you're paying yourself a little pay it won't impact your life outside of work.

4. Know Your Personal Financial Goals

You will most likely leave your business perfectly healthy if you have indisputably portrayed targets for your own records going in. These are specific from any business goals and should simply reflect what you require your own record to take after.

Individual financial goals may set aside enough emergency money to suit your family for a year or progressing in the direction of retirement. Perceiving what you require from your own records will empower you to structure the cash streams from your business in the best way that is accessible.

5. Talk to Professionals

Despite what your business looks like or what your fiscal destinations may be, it's always useful to chat with a specialist on cash related matters.

Various agents don't make the walk of chatting with budgetary coordinators, as they don't confide in them and don't have enough time. Really, it puts aside the chance to banter with a specialist and make a budgetary course of action (everything considered, dealing with money is their headliner for the duration of the day). Considering that a better than average cash related course of action can mean the refinement among security and losing everything, there's no strong reason not to take a few hours to banter with a specialist and consider at any rate working with them to prepare for most cynical situation circumstances.

Regardless, I've by and large been a vigorous understudy of individual budgetary commitment and transforming into a social entrepreneur who stood up to a sketchy fiscal destiny, joined with straying into the red, left me centered.

6. Build an emergency spare.

For a social entrepreneur, this is the correct inverse thing you can oversee. Exactly when your very own budgetary situation is placed in threat, so too is your association. Notwithstanding whether you are correct currently investigating the inventive waters or plan to take the hop later on, guarantee you build up your very own emergency spares.

7. Crowdfund

Many individuals dispatch crowd funding efforts too soon with too little arrangement and ask why they fall flat. Before you dispatch your battle, you should know precisely how much cash you'll have to dispatch your social enterprise and what the last item will resemble. These are things that you ought to have investigated through your marketable strategy rivalry and refined through a quickening agent program.

For a specific product by a social entrepreneur, being prepared to crowd fund implied inquiring about customers, forecasters and market surveyors etc. to make sense of precisely the amount he/she will have to crowd fund for our first assembling run. We at that point made a model with the goal that the majority of our funders could get a feeling of precisely what they would get when they chose that specific product. They likewise spent around a couple months arranging our battle.

You can crowd fund a great many dollars in a short measure of time on the off chance that you put in the correct measure of arranging forthright. For best practices, look at Kickstarter and Indiegogo and, for some insider tips, see Mike Del Ponte's presently great "Hacking Kickstarter."

In all probability your first funders will be your loved ones and, ideally, your freshly discovered supporters from your quickening agent program. After those systems are tapped, on the off chance that you plan your crowdfunding effort right and offer some cool advantages for giving, there is a decent possibility that the group will come through.

8. Get a credit

After you've propelled your business with a crowd funding effort and conveyed a marvellous item to every one of your patrons, you will come up short on cash. In all probability, you'll be too soon organized for financial specialists and have tapped out loved one's commitments with your crowd funding effort. I will simply go ahead and say it — I Cherish Kiva's new Kiva Zip. Through Kiva Zip, social business visionaries can get a zero-intrigue advance of $5,000 to $20,000 in only half a month. Full exposure: In the wake of being rejected by numerous banks, they raised a $5,000 advance on Kiva (the most extreme considered a first-time borrower). In the wake of paying that advance back, we simply raised another $10,000.

Not exclusively does Kiva offer zero-intrigue credits, yet it likewise gives access to a drew in system of loan specialists with a high potential to end up future clients. The drawback, obviously, is that $5,000 probably won't take you that far. For bigger strategies for financing, investigate SBA and network bank advances or less customary, fresher techniques like Accion and Loaning Club.

9. Don't surrender

I had a minute a year ago where I nearly quit. I was investing all my energy running from espresso gatherings to pitch occasions to systems administration upbeat hours with nothing to appear for it. At that point, out of nowhere, I got a call from one of my old companions, who I had worked with before and who was a noteworthy motivation behind my beginning my social enterprise. That short telephone call grounded me in the reason behind the majority of my raising support tribulations.

The astounding thing about beginning a social enterprise is that you aren't doing it for yourself. You're doing it in light of the fact that the world needs it. In this way, keep your button up, work your butt off and always remember your motivation.

ANGEL INVESTORS ARE A MAJOR SOLUTION TO FUNDING SOCIAL ENTERPRISES

Some social enterprises can earn a profit that is sufficient to get the business funded by investors. They might provide goods and services to customers willing to pay a premium for a socially beneficial product— green energy, say, or organic food. They might sell an essential service to poor customers at a decent profit while still providing that service more affordably than other suppliers do.

But many, if not most, social enterprises cannot fund themselves entirely through sales or investment. They are not profitable enough to access traditional financial markets, resulting in a financial-social return gap. The social value of providing poor people with affordable health care, basic foodstuffs, or safe cleaning products is enormous, but the cost of private funding often outweighs the monetary return.

Many social enterprises survive only through the largesse of government subsidies, charitable foundations, and a handful of high-net-worth individuals who will make donations or accept lower financial returns on their investments in social projects. The ability of those enterprises to provide their products and services rises or falls with the availability of capital from these sources, and their fundraising efforts consume time and energy that could be spent on their social missions.

The lack of funding opportunities is one of the major disadvantages' social enterprises face. A conventional business can use its balance sheet and business plan to offer different combinations of risk and return to many different types of investors: equity investors, banks, bond funds, venture capitalists, and so on.

Not so for many social enterprises—but that is changing. An increasing number of social entrepreneurs and investors are coming to realize that social enterprises of all sorts can also generate financial returns that will make them attractive to the right investors. This realization will dramatically increase the amount of capital available to these organizations.

Essentially, the insight is that you can treat the

funding of a social enterprise as a problem of financial structuring: The enterprise can offer different risks and returns to different kinds of investors instead of delivering a blended return that holds for all investors but is acceptable to very few. This new approach to structuring can close the financial-social return gap.

A growing number of social entrepreneurs and investors realize that social enterprises of all sorts can generate financial returns that will make them attractive to the right investors.

SOCIAL ENTERPRISE'S NEW BALANCE SHEET

To see how the process works, imagine that a social enterprise operating in Africa requires an investment of $100,000 to build new health clinics and expects the clinics to earn $5,000 a year—a return of 5% on the investment.

Unfortunately, 5% is too low to attract private sources of capital. Traditionally the enterprise would obtain the $100,000 from a charitable foundation instead. But suppose the enterprise asked the donor for only $50,000. It could then offer a financial investor a 10% return on the remaining $50,000. The donor would receive no repayment—but it would have $50,000 to give to another socially worthy enterprise.

You can think of a charitable donation as an investment, just as debt and equity are investments. The difference is that the return on the donation is not financial. The donor does not expect to get its money back; it expects its money to generate a social benefit. It considers the investment a failure only if that social benefit is not created.

And with a donor-investor willing to subsidize half the cost, the social enterprise becomes valuable and less risky to conventional investors. The traditional model of social enterprise leaves this value on the table. Donors lose out because they fully subsidize a project that could have attracted investment capital, and investors do not participate at all.

What we've just described is, of course, analogous to the way conventional companies are financed. By raising a portion of the capital, it needs from equity investors, a risky business can then borrow money from debt investors who seek predictable returns.

In the emerging model of social enterprise capital markets, donors play the role of equity holders, providing capital that supports an enterprise and that makes the debt taken on by financial investors safer, with better expected returns. Let's look at the tools that are taking social enterprises in this direction.

FINANCING SOCIAL ENTERPRISES

Some of the more forward-thinking foundations and social investors have realized that the current methods of financing social enterprises are inefficient, for the enterprises and themselves, and have started working to broaden the access to capital. Here are some of the mechanisms they're employing.

LOAN GUARANTEES.

The Bill & Melinda Gates Foundation now issues loan guarantees, rather than direct funds, to some of the enterprises it supports, recognizing that this is an efficient way to leverage its donations and provide organizations with more-certain funding. Its first guarantee allowed a charter school in Houston to raise $67 million in commercial debt at a low rate, saving the school (and its donors) almost $10 million in interest payments.

QUASI-EQUITY DEBT.

Some organizations have developed financial vehicles that combine the properties of equity and debt. A quasi-equity debt security is particularly useful for enterprises that are legally structured as nonprofits and therefore cannot obtain equity capital.

Such a security is technically a form of debt, but it has an important characteristic of an equity investment: Its returns are indexed to the organization's financial performance. The security holder does not have a direct claim on the governance and ownership of the enterprise, but the terms and conditions of the loan are carefully designed to give management incentives to operate the organization efficiently.

Social investors purchase these securities, which perform the function of equity and make it possible for social enterprises to offer banks and other profit-seeking lenders a competitive investment opportunity.

Consider the Bridges Social Entrepreneurs Fund—

one of several social funds of the UK investment company Bridges Ventures. The fund has some £12 million to invest in social enterprises. Recently it committed £1 million to a social loan to HCT, a company that uses surpluses from its commercial London buses, school buses, and Park & Ride services to provide community transportation for people unable to use conventional public transportation.

This social loan has a quasi-equity feature: The fund takes a percentage of revenues, thereby sharing some of the business risk and gains. Because the loan is tied to the top revenue line, it provides HCT with strong incentives to manage the business efficiently. Covenants on such loans are often added to avoid mission drift from the social goals.

Pooling.

Techniques that involve pooling funds have also opened new financial doors to social enterprises, because the pooling institution can tailor its liabilities to the needs of different kinds of investors. The Switzerland-based social capital investor Blue Orchard, for example, assembles portfolios from many micro lenders and bundles them into three tranches. The bottom tranche is Blue Orchard's equity, which offers high returns but takes the first loss.

The next tranche offers a lower expected return but has less risk. It takes the second loss, after equity is wiped out, and is analogous to a convertible bond. The top tranche promises a low but relatively safe return; it is purchased by conventional debt investors. The pooling model has spread globally, with innovators such as IFMR Trust, in Chennai, engaged in the securitization and structured finance of microfinance loan portfolios in which they retain an investment share.

SOCIAL IMPACT BONDS.

Another innovation, the social impact bond, deserves special notice for its ability to help governments fund infrastructure and services, especially as public budgets are cut and municipal bond markets are stressed. Launched in the UK in 2010, this type of bond is sold to private investors who are paid a return only if the public project succeeds—if, say, a rehabilitation program lowers the rate of recidivism among newly released prisoners. It allows private investors to do what they do best: take calculated risks in pursuit of profits.

The government, for its part, pays a fixed return to investors for verifiable results and keeps any additional savings. Because it shifts the risk of program failure from taxpayers to investors, this mechanism has the potential to transform political discussions about expanding social services.

From the U.S. to Australia, national and local governments are developing pilot bonds to fund interventions targeting homelessness, early childhood education, and other issues. The U.S. could even use this approach to support its finance-starved space program— for instance, issuing "space bonds" that would pay a return only if a manned mission were to reach Mars on schedule and under budget.

Developments like these are stretching the boundaries of social enterprise financing. It isn't hard to imagine that at some point social enterprises will have an even broader universe of funding options than conventional businesses do. If you think of charitable donations as a form of investment, and if an appropriate legal structure is created, then you have, by definition, a new class of investors and a new type of return (see the exhibit "Financing Social Enterprises").

An organization delivering a social return could obtain seed capital from donors without giving the donors any claim on assets. The seed capital could then be augmented by equity capital with a residual claim on assets and by debt capital with a prior claim on assets and cash flow. With all these types of liabilities available and with the possibility of securitizing and selling them, the funding and growth possibilities for social enterprises start to look very promising indeed.

And the benefits aren't limited to social enterprises; financial markets stand to gain, too. The emerging model broadens the range of asset classes investors can tap to diversify their portfolios. Investors can now obtain returns from completely new sets of products and customer groups, often in new countries. This is precisely why securitized bonds issued against microloans proved so popular.

MAKING IT HAPPEN

If the financial crisis taught us one thing, it's that the machinery and infrastructure of financial markets matter a lot. Without standards and ratings, investors can't distinguish between good investments and bad ones, and lawmakers can't provide frameworks to regulate and protect investors and companies alike.

When it comes to evaluating a social enterprise, the challenge is doubled. In many areas the market machinery and infrastructure for evaluating social risks and returns are barely developed. This can have two effects: It can starve good organizations of funding and leave investors focused solely on financial returns.

As Harvard Business School's Robert Kaplan and Allen Grossman argued in these pages, investments in social causes will remain chronically inefficient unless the social sector comes up with transparent ways to measure, report, and monitor social outcomes. Recognizing the need for such transparency, the Rockefeller Foundation joined with many of the most important social venture investors in launching a major effort to finance the development of institutional machinery and infrastructure for social enterprise capital markets.

Part of this effort involved the creation, in 2009, of

a nonprofit called the Global Impact Investing Network. One of the organization's first initiatives was the Impact Reporting and Investment Standards (IRIS) project, which seeks to establish criteria for double-bottom-line investing, where the first line is financial, and the second line is social. What, for example, is the right way to measure childhood literacy? For an enterprise involved in primary education, the second line might be the number of children enrolled in schools, or how many can read. By specifying what items should appear on the second line, IRIS has taken the first step toward the development of common standards for reporting social outcomes—just as GAAP provides a common language for comparing investment options.

Greater precision and transparency with respect to social outcomes will make it easier to disentangle the social returns and risks of a blended business from the financial ones. This in turn will allow a social enterprise and its investors to determine the appropriate balance between charitable and non-charitable capital, and from there the enterprise can use the machinery and infrastructure of the financial markets to the fullest. All parties will benefit.

Donors will be able to leverage their gifts to support more activities, and they will be better able to assess the effectiveness of their donations. Social enterprises will have access to the capital they need for growth consistent with their social missions. Financial investors will have a hugely expanded range of investment opportunities.

Let us be clear: We do not underestimate the challenges involved in creating fully functioning capital markets and legal frameworks to serve social enterprises. It's hard enough creating them to serve for-profit entities that do not have social missions. We also recognize that some of the innovations we've discussed will not be suitable for all organizations. We need to figure out how to sustain those organizations as well. But with the right market infrastructure and legal framework in place, enormous amounts of private capital could be mobilized for social enterprises.

In the United States alone, charitable foundations hold $600 billion in investment assets but donate less than $50 billion each year. Effective financial engineering could unlock those endowment assets and also attract some of the trillions of dollars currently held in mainstream portfolios. The ability to tap these deep pools of capital will be a significant contribution to creating a greener, healthier, and more equitable world.

LEARN HOW TO HANDLE COMPLACENCY

Complacency is one of the greatest dangers to progress.

It resembles a plaque which should be destroyed before it hurts you. It makes you generally need to remain at the safe place and excessively terrified, making it impossible to use the possibility to the more elevated amount in view of having negative reasoning on committing errors, going out on a limb and confronting disappointments.

Call attention to one fruitful individual in this world who has achieved an exceptional accomplishment in complacency? Indeed, you can't discover any. Enormous names, for example, Sir Richard Branson, the late Steve Jobs, Bill Gates, Donald Trump, Robert Kiyosaki, Jack Ma, Oprah Winfrey, Carlos Slim Helu, Warren Buffet, Akio Morita - Founder of Sony, Jimmy Choo and numerous more around the world, have removed their complacency mind and agreeable seat to confront challenges and more serious hazard for their identity now.

Smug individuals love to remain clearly at all the time in self-satisfied climate. They are one of lethal sorts of individuals to my feeling. On the off chance that you are the constructive kind of social business visionary, you ought to keep away from this gathering of individuals since they have 'undesirable radiation'. It is difficult to make dynamic strides to progress with this 'species' since they will turn out with too many negative considerations, reasons and thinking not to be separated of most noteworthy difficulties. Be that as it may, amusingly, they are anticipating take the compliment and examination of any simple achievement comes crossing their direction.

Complacency can 'murder' you from getting to be imaginative and inventive. The majority of circumstances, smug individuals will just investigate 'alternate ways', most effortless and quickest approach to achieve something. This sort of attitude will never know how to fundamentally think. Life dependably begins toward the finish of your customary range of familiarity. You will never develop and pick up anything about the juice of life on the off chance that you are surrendered to complacency.

The individuals who make history and novel in their achievement never begin with complacency. Hardship, difficulties and turbulences will create you to have solid positive character, more shrewd, howdy opposition, basic personality, industriousness, ending up more inventive and imaginative manner in which you see things throughout everyday life.

Complacency can be the absolute most perilous danger to any business and a social enterprise visionary. Like runaway tree roots, complacency grabs hold of an association's way of life, and the most exceedingly terrible part is, in numerous organizations, initiative is either ease back to remember it or does nothing to stop it.

At the point when complacency grabs hold of a social enterprise person or a business, the accompanying results can turn out to be genuine:

- You lose your focused edge.

- You start to frequently endure average execution.

- Your rivalry gets more grounded and quicker than you, picking up piece of the pie without you notwithstanding acknowledging, until it is past the point of no return.

- You not just lose your better entertainers, since they are not being tested, but rather you are likewise unfit to draw in new ability.

- You lose clients, cash and in the end your business.

At the point when the authority of an association or social entrepreneur ends up careless, they are likely additionally succumbing to inheritance considering.

Their complacency makes them be hesitant to challenge business as usual on the grounds that they are "agreeable" with where they are. The outcome is that they are situating themselves and their association for a future calamity.

They erroneously feel that their present existing conditions will proceed into the future "as seems to be." Legacy thinking shows itself in phrases like "that is the manner in which we generally do it," "it worked fine last time" or my top choice, "in the event that it ain't broke, don't fix it."

So, what's the answer for ward off the danger of complacency and stay away from inheritance considering? The arrangement begins with you, the pioneer, the social entrepreneur, and your perspectives and propensities toward your very own advancement. Why? Since the basic actuality is, the point at which you, the social business person, show signs of improvement, your group and your business will take after. Personal growth is a standout amongst other counteracts ants to ward off complacency.

Social entrepreneurs that support "considering" at all levels have the most obvious opportunity to evade the risky impacts of complacency inside their association.

Here are twelve basic strides to kick you off the correct way:

1. Be sure about your long-term vision (close to two

years out) and your transient objectives expected to make that vision a reality.

Clearness will enable you to set the correct desires and guide your group to take the correct activities. Dealing with the correct things keeps complacency outside of the doors.

2. Have a particular arrangement for every day. Spotlight on the most imperative undertakings first— the ones that are straightforwardly identified with your objectives and vision.

3. Give yourself particular time every week—close to 60 minutes—to think deliberately and assess where you are and, in the event, that you are heading the correct way.

In this "meeting with yourself," question your own business as usual. Be fiercely genuine in your evaluation of how things are completing.

4. Test your group to think.

Try not to be hesitant to request their input. Make inquiries about what they are doing. Do they know why they do it? Furthermore, do they have any recommendations on the most proficient method to improve?

5. Empower and reward advancement. Your groups for the most part have the best answers for enhance efficiency, administration and results. A decent companion once revealed to me an account of an organization that gave

out an honour for "the best most exceedingly bad thought" just to urge their group to consider better approaches to get things done.

6. Make a formal procedure to gain from botches. By realizing what you could have done any other way, you challenge your group to think and maintain a strategic distance from heritage considering.

7. At last, contribute time and cash to enhance your aptitudes and information. What's more, that incorporates the aptitudes and information of your group. Personal growth is extraordinary compared to other cures to ward off complacency.

The best pioneers urge their groups to consider how to challenge the present state of affairs and search for approaches to improve the situation consistently. It is to a great degree uncommon that an organization that considers and follows up on an opportune premise—to a limited extent by utilizing the above advances—will ever succumb to complacency.

8. Figure out how to delegate! When you make sense of how to give up and enable other individuals to help you as a social business person, you open a great deal more important time to direct the ship, which is for what reason you're a business person in any case. Designating can be extremely hard for a few people, yet endeavor to enhance it and you will discover an expansion in efficiency.

9. Getting to be careless. Getting careless,

notwithstanding for a moment. Complacency is the adversary of business/social enterprise. You can't develop actually or professionally except if you're tested. Dialling your inspiration back can have an enduring negative effect, and at whatever point I've wound up in periods of it, I've generally thought back with lament.

10. Be readied. Put yourself through a "For Dummies" compressed lesson or comparable. You have to know how to peruse fundamental money related explanations and comprehend center straightforward bookkeeping ideas (money versus gathering premise) as a social business person. The rest becomes alright once you have the vocabulary. Confiding in your instinct joined with money related education can take you far first and foremost, yet past a specific point, you need to utilize experts to make sense of these subtle elements for you. At any rate you'll have the capacity to talk their dialect.

11. Allow Others To Have Influence. Numerous organizations and pioneers say that they need their kin to have more impact, yet they are not giving up enough. Therefore, regardless of or maybe despite their best expectations to encourage a culture of assorted masterminds, organizations as a rule try to control the execution of their workers in view of obsolete mindsets. They take no chances, fitting in with existing working environment commitment practices and cultivating that "I simply do what I am told" approach. Nobody sees or follows more than the undeniable chances. Who needs to utilize "roundabout vision" to foresee the unforeseen?

Who needs to acknowledge or focus on their kin and their individual endeavors? Everybody simply continue doing what you are told.

That is the thing that happens when different people in the room don't trust that they have the impact. I don't surmise that the official knew about the negative disturbance he was making. He thought he was sharing his viewpoint. Furthermore, he was. The issue was he was inviting assorted variety of thought and as a result he drove others down a way of complacency as he empowered the gathering towards unravelling for the wrong chances.

What this pioneer expected to do was tune in and be shrewd, helpless, and bold enough to enable others to have impact. Truly, truly, being defenseless as pioneer was seen as an indication of shortcoming. In any case, in the present business atmosphere, the speed of progress compels us as pioneers to carry others into the overlap, significantly snappier. Let be honest, nobody has every one of the appropriate responses – and when we surmise that we do, the commercial center reveals to us generally.

12. Challenge The Status Quo. Pioneers develop intelligence in others when they really regard contrasts and the individuals who upset existing conditions for the advancement of a more beneficial entire – not negative disturbance, which prompts complacency. On the off chance that we are not advancing in the correct ways then we are really augmenting the holes regardless of

whether we think we are doing the things assumed do to close them. While the official in the gathering thought he was advancing the discussion, he was accidentally constraining everybody to fall into the device of complacency. Therefore, nobody in the organization has the bravery to challenge existing conditions. He was unconsciously making strain.

This doesn't simply occur in gatherings. For instance, it happens when there is an authority change at an organization. Rather than seeing the chance to advance, they pause and look for authorization since they realize that the new supervisor will see the world uniquely in contrast to the past manager.

LEARN HOW TO JUDGE YOURSELF BY YOUR GOALS INSTEAD OF BY WHAT YOUR PEERS SEEM TO BE DOING

As a social entrepreneur you must set goals for yourself. It is now of almost importance to realise those goals. Everyone on this earth or rather in any business endeavor, you must have some set goals. Therefore, you as a social entrepreneur must set your goals and strive to realize them.

Although as a business person especially in the social enterprise it is not possible to not have friends or peers who have set goals and try to realize them. But unfortunately, many entrepreneurs make the mistaking of judging themselves by what their friends or peers seem to be doing. This is a grave foolishness as it affects their business orientation and focus.

Imaging your peers setting specific goals and you begin to think that there's better and yours is no good or that you have set poor goals and visions for yourself. This act of foolishness will definitely bring the business of the social entrepreneur down before they know what is going on.

There are certain things as a social entrepreneur that you must do based on your goals and how it affects you.

- Why you should hush up about Your Objectives
- Keep Your Huge Objective a Major Mystery
- Get Some Energy Before You Drop the News
- Naysayers Going to Naysay
- Going, Going, Gone

1. Why You Should Hush up about Your Objectives

Sharing isn't generally a smart thought. In case you're similar to the vast majority, when you have a major objective, you're likely tingling to discuss it. Energy assumes control and you need to tell everybody. It's regularly finished with the honourable expectation of considering yourself responsible to the expectations and fantasies that would somehow live quietly in your creative energy. Furthermore, by telling the world, it can feel as if you're establishing your plans into genuine activity....

Well, for reasons unknown, not genuine. None of it is. And if for some reason it doesn't go well you begin to judge yourself based on others progress.

2. Keep Your Huge Objective a Major Mystery

In any event for a smidgen in any case. It might come as a stun; however objective setting is best done in isolation. Also, racing to tell companions, collaborators, and your mother isn't such a savvy initial phase in completing the things you need to accomplish.

Studies demonstrate that sharing objectives on motivation or rashly can really diminish the probability that we'll see them into realization. Actually, simply vocalizing these plans to others triggers a sentiment of achievement; it traps your mind into supposing you've accomplished something. We subliminally feel like we've stepped toward finishing said objective, which is obviously not the situation. This misguided feeling of exertion at that point decreases our natural inspiration to really begin the genuine work and reduces the probability we'll step toward finishing the objective.

3. Get Some Energy Before You Drop the News

In case you're not kidding about an objective, you might need to cancel the presses and hold the social posts until you've gained some genuine ground with the entire undertaking.

Centre gatherings have been held since the 1930s demonstrating this hypothesis. Members who had an objective, however harboured it for a bit, had unquestionably inspiration and internal fire to make progress toward finishing their expectations. While the individuals who quickly declared their plans previously laying any preparation proceeded to wait far longer—if not uncertainly—in those basic starting stages, and at last, were far less inclined to achieve their objective.

4. Naysayers Going to Naysay

Notwithstanding deceiving yourself into supposing you've gained genuine ground, there's another killjoy to yelling your objectives from the housetops. Sharing your new objective rashly resembles putting a delicate seedling out in the brilliant sun too soon. You open your plan to the brutal suppositions of the world before it's prepared.

Rather, pause. Secure it. Truly become acquainted with it. Comprehend your objective, why you need it, and how you intend to accomplish it. Develop it, so when the time comes to begin offering it to the world, you're in a decent place to take helpful feedback, influence enhancements, to tune into important information, and unhesitatingly close down the naysayers. Since there will dependably be naysayers.

5. Going, Going, Gone

While it's imperative to keep your objectives and fantasies only for you, only for a bit, you don't need to keep your lips zipped for eternity. When you're prepared, pick a companion, tutor, or accomplice to trust in. It ought to be somebody whom you trust and whose assessment implies a lot to you not make you judge yourself according to their accomplishments. Begin to skip the objective and your thoughts off of them. Demonstrate to them where you're at and where you need to go. Gut-check everything. Perceive how things are arriving outside of your own mind. This is an energizing advance! You're putting things out into the universe. Stuff is going on. Neural connections are terminating! Perceive how they respond. Furthermore, react likewise—tweaking, tinkering, and chugging endlessly at drawing nearer to your objective.

What's more, when you're prepared, gradually yet definitely start to let whatever is left of the world in on the news. Also, grin as you watch your once minor seedling start to grow into something genuinely wonderful.

To ensure that you don't begin to judge yourself based on your peers' accomplishments and goals, it is imperative that you get your goals right and work towards them as a social entrepreneur.

• Working out your goals on paper improve your probability of objective achievement by 80%

• Defining business related goals in view of your qualities can expand your work commitment by 700%

• Be that as it may, on the off chance that you truly need to reliably meet and surpass your most critical goals throughout everyday life and work.

• It's not just about defining Shrewd Goals. You have to set Super-Brilliant Goals.

• We should begin with a speedy look how to make Savvy Objective Setting much more astute and after that module some motivational rocket fuel from the best accessible social science.

Alright so you've most likely known about the:

1 ~ Savvy Objective Setting Procedure where you set goals that are:

S-pecific

M-easurable

A-ttainable

R-elevant

T-ime Bound

- Particular means their unmistakable. On the off chance that you told another person how you characterized this objective they would rapidly and effectively comprehend what you mean.

- Quantifiable means you have a reasonable method for knowing when you finished the objective.

- Feasible implies that it's a practical objective with a solid probability you can accomplish on the off chance that you remain centred and take every necessary step.

- Important implies that achieving the objective will increase the value of life or work. For instance, worker and group goals should be significant to the general business methodology or the association.

- Time Bound implies that you set a date or time for finish. Far superior when you set particular occasions every day to deal with your goals.

- Presently there are various approaches to make Savvy Goals significantly more astute. In any case, today, allows simply centre around the most critical way - and that is called:

2 ~ Objective Behaviorization:

Objective Behaviorization (GB) really extends and fortifies the "Quantifiable" some portion of Shrewd Goals.

Not exclusively is GB the key to the world's best execution administration and gamification forms but at the same time it's the apparatus utilized by the best group pioneers, administrators and execution mentors to encourage their groups and customers reliably develop while getting the outcomes they need.

What makes GB so great as a goal setting and achievement technique?

Put basically, behaviorizing your goals really lets your module probably the most ground-breaking connected motivational science specifically into rapidly fabricating, keep up and super-rouse the practices and propensities that lead straightforwardly to your objective state as a social entrepreneur.

So how would you really utilize Objective Behaviorization, all things considered? Whenever you set a Keen objective, outline it inside the setting of the particular and at whatever point conceivable, discernible practices that are expected to achieve the objective as fast and adequately as could reasonably be expected.

These can be genuine practices, for example, coding, composing, and looking into, time spent on the circular machine or the time riding your bicycle to work.

They can likewise be advanced practices like the time a client goes through collaborating with a client encounter interface or noting question on a client created content stage like Quora.

Truth be told, a large number of the world's best organizations really behaviorize key goals that characterize their organization societies.

That way they can prepare for, measure, perceive and compensate those practices all the more adequately progressively.

Beginning to consider your goals as far as particular, quantifiable practices will frequently lead you to rapidly and effectively recognize social sub goals that you may have missed generally and not planned and finished.

So, realize that you've a solid feeling of how goal setting functions, how about we take a gander at the motivational rocket fuel to keep you engaged and roused while understand those goals - beginning with:

3 ~ Characterizing Your "Why" and Take after Your Delight's

> *"Individuals don't purchase what you do; they purchase why you do it. Furthermore, what you do just demonstrates what you accept." - Simon Sinek*

The initial phase in building large amounts of maintained inspiration and centre for accomplishing stretch or execution goals is to begin by throwing a social enterprise vision that connects them to your most profound feeling of reason - the "why" and not the how of your goals.

In case you're single most critical "why" doesn't hop out at you immediately, consider those achievements throughout your life that you extremely cherished the most - the ones that gave you the most profound sense satisfaction and bliss doing them and accomplishing them.

Here's initiative and self-awareness Jedi Simon Sinek's clarification of your why:

Pioneers and chiefs on the planet's most productive and imaginative organizations see consistently bridle the interminable motivational intensity of "why".

Characterizing you for what reason is one of

143

the first and most imperative methodologies new Google administrators at instructed in their initiative improvement preparing. They utilize it to fuel the most elevated amounts of commitment and execution in their groups through instructing.

Truth be told, ongoing exploration demonstrates that defining goals that straightforwardly satisfy or connection to the satisfaction of a profound feeling of design, is currently more compelling than money related pay as the best wellspring of employment fulfilment.

4 ~Module Uplifting feedback - The Cool Combination Like - Unending Wellspring of Extraordinary Inspiration.

With regards to objective Behaviorization, the absolute most intense instrument available to you is Uplifting feedback (PR).

To the extent quick cerebrum-based conduct change and propensity arrangement goes, PR has been appeared to be more successful than intellectual treatment or prescription for treating clinical melancholy. It additionally speaks to the best in class in high-return for capital invested execution administration frameworks and the world's best information driven gamification programs.

By its extreme definition; Encouraging feedback actually can't neglect to get staggering outcomes when legitimately connected.

Why?

Indeed, in light of the fact that it's characterized as:

Any discernible occasion that takes after a conduct, and, that expands the event/quality of that conduct next time in a comparative or indistinguishable circumstance.

Presently even once you've defined Super-Savvy Goals, connected to the most profound and best wellsprings of inspiration to realize them - snags and difficulties may at present emerge.

At the point when things get extremely intense, this is the place you have to in a general sense focus on making even the following littlest stride conceivable subsequent stage towards your objective state as a social enterprise.

Try not to overpower yourself with the bigger objective when you're as of now over-burden or over-focused.

Truly simply centre on the following straightforward conduct, and I mean truly the following physical advance for some mission basic goals, until the point that you increase positive social force once more.

Step by step instructions on how to judge yourself based on your goals

Not all goals justify keeping. Here's simply the way by which to release from one more Year's objective that shows up on your summary again and again.

In the event that you're in the inclination for making New Year's objectives, you may see that, after some time, the once-over ends up being peculiarly normal. Notwithstanding you're endeavouring to lose a comparable 10 lb. or on the other hand entire your degree or start that business. Extremely, this could be the year it happens, yet envision a situation in which you pick it isn't. By what method may you let go of a whole deal objective with your certainty perfect?

"It's incredible that we dither about giving up targets," says Influence Nease, past supervisor scientist at Express Substance and author of the normal book The Power of Fifty Bits: The New Investigation of Changing Benevolent designs into Positive Results. "In case we let go too quickly, we let go of the opportunity to shock ourselves and do things we didn't figure we could do."

If the target genuinely doesn't suit your life any more, and it's pushed toward getting to be something that you use to feel dreadful about yourself, keeping the goal isn't serving anyone.

Everything considered, fault is an inclination best put something aside for precedents when you've truly hurt someone. "I'm for keeping your announcement, anyway in case the target genuinely doesn't oblige your life any more, and it's advanced toward getting to be something that you use to feel frightful about yourself, keeping the goal isn't serving anyone, specifically you," says Kate Hanley, author of the normal book A Period of Consistently Calm.

Here are five distinctive approaches to give up a goal while so far enjoying you:

1. Pick the goal isn't yours

Consider why you set your target. If you have to get a degree since you welcome the subject and figure it will support your employment, which is phenomenal. If this is in light of the fact that each other individual you know has an equivalent degree and you accept they're settling on a choice about you, "I'd battle that your goal isn't self-pushed. It's proposed to keep others happy, and you genuinely don't have control over others' happiness," says Hanley. Life is too short to condemn yourself according to others' wants. Focus on the goals you've set since they matter to you and not what others do as. A social entrepreneur

2. Put it on the sooner or later rundown

I venerate effectiveness ace David Allen's idea of an "at some point later on/maybe" list. It's a not too bad place to stop destinations that sound drawing in, yet may not be legitimate for your recurring pattern time of life in a social enterprise. I've run one marathon, and possibly sooner or later I'll run another, anyway for the present, half-marathons are significantly less requesting to fit into a schedule that incorporates working throughout the day and contemplating four little youths.

3. Consider what you'd tell a friend

"People with everything taken into account are substantially harder on themselves than on different people," says Nease. So, plot the issue thusly: "if it were my nearest partner who was having this same issue, what may I let him know?" Regardless of whether he was surrendering the goal of hinting at change work since he confided in no one would acquire someone like him, you'd work to encourage his assurance and teach him to keep endeavouring. Be that as it may, in case he was making himself miserable in light of the way that he quantified 10 lb. more than in auxiliary school, you'd probably told him not to make such a noteworthy experience about it. You could unveil to yourself a comparable thing.

In case you'd prompt your nearest buddy not to make such a noteworthy experience about it, you can uncover to yourself a comparative thing not forgetting you're a social entrepreneur.

4. Think nearly nothing

Little wins are to a great degree motivational. So, while the likelihood of "gigantic shaggy bold destinations" (to refer to Jim Collins) still has its supporters, you ought to truly think about slanting toward the soundness that you are purposefully giving up immense targets for more diminutive, to a great degree reachable goal. You're not going to meet your ideal accomplice this year, if you're not intending to go on more dates and meet new people. "Better to back off a bit and shoot low, and after that ratchet up as you succeed, instead of shoot high and ratchet down," says Nease. "That is extremely troublesome."

5. Focus on frames

Finally, destinations are no doubt overstated. "We may contribute unreasonably vitality thinking about targets," says Nease. "What is critical is rehearses. That is the thing that gets us to destinations." instead of characterizing a goal to lose 10 lb., you set a target to eat 5 servings of vegetables every day and exercise for 30 minutes 4 times every week. Conceivably you'll get fit as a fiddle and maybe you won't, yet you'll irrefutably be more useful, which ideally was your motivation for getting more fit regardless of you been a social entrepreneur.

Stop settling on a choice about Yourself In perspective of others individual's Goals

All things considered, here are a few things you can do.

1) Evacuate Diversions.

When my dad was contending to wind up an expert gamer, he never stared at the television. Ever, s I promise to you, I have no clue what demonstrates were well known somewhere in the range of 2004 and 2008 on the grounds that he cut out TV and different thoughtless diversions to give him more opportunity to work on gaming. Evacuating diversions is fundamental.

Meaning you are able to diverse your peers and other goals as a social entrepreneur.

2) Record Your Objectives

In short: Record what you need to achieve, both long haul and here and now. Every day, your undertaking rundown ought to move in the direction of those goals and objectives and not others goal and objectives. In the event that it's not, at that point it's anything but difficult to see where you are investing your energy, so you can straighten out.

3) Measure

"In the event that you can't gauge it, don't do it." - Ron Gibori

When you set a goal, make sense of how you will measure achievement. Is it just finishing the undertaking? Is it collecting a specific measure of cash? Is it what number of individuals see it or perused it? Set a quantifiable objective, track it, and be straightforward with the outcome. It's the main way you'll develop yourself and your social enterprise.

4) Feed Your Mind

You need to contemplate your art. On the off chance that you need to begin your own organization, read about different organizations, read contextual analyses, inquire about your industry and contending businesses. Read the examples of overcoming adversity for inspiration and read the defeats for point of view. The more you read and study, the more honed your tool compartment will be and your resolve to not judge yourself base on other goals.

5) Encircle Yourself with Great Individuals

General guideline: The 5 individuals you invest the most energy with are an impression of you. In the event that you encircle yourself with individuals that are shrewd, determined workers, enthusiastic about what they do, at that point those characteristics will rub off on you. In case you're the most astute person in the room, you should clear out. You'll just end up judging yourself based on others achievement.

6) Exercise

A consistent theme between incredible personalities is work out. Regardless of whether it's a game, heading off to the rec centre, or taking a lively stroll through the recreation centre, being tuned in to your body will enable you to get past the psychological marathons required to deliver awesome work and accomplish your goals.

7) Think

To those that are new to this training, I understand it appears to be irregular. As approval, I'd get a kick out of the chance to advise you that DaVinci, Tesla, Occupations, and so on all credited contemplation to their splendid thoughts. Take some time toward the beginning of the day and around evening time before bed to calm your psyche and let the inventiveness come to you—rather than you constantly pursuing it.

8) Evacuate Your Indecencies

This is not quite the same as expelling diversions. Diversions are the television, mobile phone, the gathering adjacent, and so forth. Indecencies are the things we utilize when we incredibly need to stay away from the diligent work. By evacuating them, we can turn out to be more mindful of what inside us is keeping us down. I guarantee you, in the event that you are a consumer, a smoker, what have you, and you evacuate it, you will see very obviously the minutes when you long for it and the minutes when you (shockingly) have no hankering by any means. What's more, those desires will give you universes of understanding to what really keeps you away from accomplishing enormity.

9) Love

Being infatuated is dependably a sure-fire approach to getting propelled to achieve extraordinary things. In any case, love can likewise be felt outside of a close relationship. Like investing energy with great individuals, discover approaches to genuinely convey what needs be with individuals you feel good with. Make some time, regardless of how little, to invest energy with family and companions amid your work week instead of comparing yourself. Indeed, even the world's best social entrepreneur require embraces sometimes.

10) Dispose Of The Refuse

This is, as I would see it, the most imperative piece of being laser centred on your goals. Set aside a few minutes TO PLAY! In the event that you are a painter, don't spend each day painting all genuinely. On the off chance that you are an author, don't spend each day slaving without end on your novel. Get that guitar sitting toward the edge of your room, go construct a $10 demonstrate auto one evening, get that plastic lightsaber in your wardrobe and go fight your more youthful sibling in the lawn—I mean, on Tatooine. Do the senseless easily overlooked details that assistance the cerebrum recall that all imagination assumed be enjoyable. Objectives as large as the sun won't be accomplished regardless of how quick you attempt to dash down the way. You need to fly, old buddy. Also, you fly when the trash in your mind is gone, and you recall that you're doing what you adore and push out the thought of comparing or judging yourself based on others goals and accomplishments.

Judging yourself based on other people's goals and accomplishment is such a killjoy and leaves a very unfortunate and negative effect on the entrepreneurs' goals involving the business or social enterprises.

JAMES JAY MAWAKA

CONCLUSION

When you follow the business impact brand methodology in building your social enterprise, your social enterprise is sure to scale and become a global phenomenon. In the meantime, thank you for the commitment to learning, to being a practitioner and allowing me to share the tools and methods that have made a difference in my life and those I serve. Always dedicate yourself, not only to strive for the business goals you have set, but to meet your personal goals too. Dream bigger than before and make the world a better place than you found it, live and give generously.

Congratulations on completing this book and see you at the top.

NOTES

ABOUT LENOIR FOUNDATION

LeNoir Foundation is a nonprofit organisation driven by a single goal; to do our part in making the world a better place for all. We are specifically focused on providing relief to poor, distressed, and underprivileged children residing in Zimbabwe, Uganda and India by developing academic scholarships and educational programs. We lovingly extend our hands to those in need to provide excellent, life-changing opportunities. In addition, we strive to prepare them so that they may overcome daily challenges and receive a better future.

A vision realised

The foundation has been a lifelong dream come true for Jay. A committed philanthropist who believes life is a gift and all of us who have the ability must remember that we have the responsibility to give something back. Your contributions can truly make a difference.

Leaders Sponsorship Programme

Among the foundation's most inspiring endeavors is the "Leaders" Sponsorship Programme. Having spent time in Africa, Jay was instantly taken by the number of children without access to basic education. He has since dedicated his life to building LeNoir foundation, to ensure that the poorest and vulnerable will receive an education. Currently the foundation sponsor's 10 primary school students and participates in many other philanthropic endeavors. Please join us as we are actively seeking new sponsors to enable a new group of children to begin primary school in January 2020.

If you would like to make a difference in this way, please email: info@lenoirfoundation.com and we'll send you a sponsorship form.

WWW.LENOIRFOUNDATION.COM

ABOUT THE AUTHOR

Born in Bulawayo, Zimbabwe, Jay moved to the United Kingdom as an adolescent. Not only was he forced to learn a new culture and an entirely different way of life, Jay searched for his true calling while earning a degree from London South Bank University. It was there he discovered he was a true social entrepreneur. Passionate about solving injustice and inequality, he now dedicates his time and energy to overcoming deep-rooted problems holding back progress.

The LeNoir Foundation is his gift to others. Jay founded this organization to allow today's youth to build upon their education while providing emotional support necessary to develop their full potential. Jay's love for economic empowerment, the LeNoir Foundation has numerous innovative educational programs aimed at improving the quality of life for our youth. These programs are carried out in conjunction with local schools in Zimbabwe and India.

Jay cites his strongest source of motivation is his vision for the future, not only for himself, but his family and the surrounding communities. When not enriching the lives of others, Jay enjoys reading, running marathons, public speaking through Toastmasters, and traveling. His belief is if you don't read you won't gain the information, insight, and inspiration to make the right calls at the right time.

You can learn more about Jay and the LeNoir Foundation here: www.lenoirfoundation.com

Printed in Great Britain
by Amazon